CORNELIUS

A Business Affair in Three Transactions

BY

J. B. PRIESTLEY

Copyright, 1935, by J. B. Priestley
Copyright (Acting Edition), 1936, by J. B. Priestley

All rights reserved

SAMUEL FRENCH, LTD.
26 Southampton Street, Strand, London, W.C.2
59 Cross Street, Manchester
SAMUEL FRENCH, INC.
25 West 45th Street, New York, U.S.A.
811 West 7th Street, Los Angeles, Cal.
SAMUEL FRENCH (CANADA), LTD.
480 University Avenue, Toronto

Copyright © 1935 by J.B. Priestley
Copyright (Acting Edition) © 1936 by J.B. Priestley
All Rights Reserved

CORNELIUS is fully protected under the copyright laws of the British Commonwealth, including Canada, the United States of America, and all other countries of the Copyright Union. All rights, including professional and amateur stage productions, recitation, lecturing, public reading, motion picture, radio broadcasting, television and the rights of translation into foreign languages are strictly reserved.

ISBN 978-0-573-11649-0

www.samuelfrench.co.uk
www.samuelfrench.com

For Amateur Production Enquiries

United Kingdom and World
excluding north america
plays@samuelfrench.co.uk
020 7255 4302/01

Each title is subject to availability from Samuel French, depending upon country of performance.

CAUTION: Professional and amateur producers are hereby warned that CORNELIUS is subject to a licensing fee. Publication of this play does not imply availability for performance. Both amateurs and professionals considering a production are strongly advised to apply to the appropriate agent before starting rehearsals, advertising, or booking a theatre. A licensing fee must be paid whether the title is presented for charity or gain and whether or not admission is charged.

The Professional Rights in this play are controlled by United Agents LLP, 12-26 Lexington Street, London W1F 0LE.

No one shall make any changes in this title for the purpose of production. No part of this book may be reproduced, stored in a retrieval system, or transmitted in any form, by any means, now known or yet to be invented, including mechanical, electronic, photocopying, recording, videotaping, or otherwise, without the prior written permission of the publisher. No one shall upload this title, or part of this title, to any social media websites.

The right of J.B. Priestley to be identified as author of this work has been asserted in accordance with Section 77 of the Copyright, Designs and Patents Act 1988.

CORNELIUS

Produced at the Duchess Theatre, London, W.C.2, on March 20th, 1935, with the following cast of characters:

(In the order of their appearance)

MRS. ROBERTS	*Muriel George.*
LAWRENCE	*Tom Gill.*
MISS PORRIN	*Ann Wilton.*
BIDDLE	*James Harcourt.*
CORNELIUS	*Ralph Richardson.*
RUG MAN	*Albert Ward.*
ERIC SHEFFORD	*William Rodwell.*
PAPER TOWEL MAN	*Paul Smythe.*
COLEMAN	*Felix Irwin.*
YOUNG WOMAN	*Hazel Carnegie.*
EX-OFFICER	*Raymond Huntley.*
JUDY EVISON	*Victoria Hopper.*
DR. SCHWEIG	*Felix Irwin.*
FLETCHER	*Raymond Huntley.*
ELDERLY MAN	*Albert Ward.*
MRS. READE	*Dorothy Hamilton.*
PRITCHET .	*Victor Tandy.*
MORTIMER	*Robert Gilbert.*
THREE CREDITORS	{ *Paul Smythe.* *Robin May.* *Arthur Howard.*
ROBERT MURRISON	*Harcourt Williams.*

Play Produced by BASIL DEAN.

SYNOPSIS OF SCENERY

The action takes place in the General Office of Briggs and Murrison, Birdcage Street, Holborn.

ACT I
Monday Morning.

ACT II
Wednesday Afternoon.

ACT III
Friday Evening. Two Weeks later.

[Photograph by Stage Photo Co.

To face page 5]

CORNELIUS

ACT I

SCENE.—*The Office of Messrs. Briggs & Murrison, aluminium importers, Birdcage Street, Holborn. Monday morning.*

An ordinary general office room of the more old-fashioned kind, with a recess at the back lit by opaque window in the wall. Window to street on L., *main door on* L. *at right angles to window. On right wall, door to Private Office. Two desks in recess at back, one of them with a typewriter and a telephone. Small table with typewriter and typist's chair in front of window on* L. *Copying-in corner by recess on* R. *Ledgers, files, etc., prominent on walls.*

(*See Photograph of Scene.*)

When CURTAIN *rises, the office is empty. There is a pale wintry sunshine coming through window on* L. *Then private office door opens, and* MRS. ROBERTS *backs out, followed by gusts of smoke. She coughs and angrily mutters:* " Oh, blast the thing ! " *then goes back into the room. She is a stoutish Cockney woman in her fifties, with a red face, a hoarse voice, and a ripe character.* LAWRENCE *enters* L., *a rather weedy youth of nineteen, wearing a raincoat that is not very adequate for this cold weather. He blows on his hands, then sees* MRS. ROBERTS *coming out of the private office again, followed by smoke.*

LAWRENCE (*taking letters out of the basket on the door*). Hello, you're late.

MRS. ROBERTS. Yes, and you'd be late if you'd that devil of a thing in there to deal with. (*She backs to* R.C., *coughing.*)

LAWRENCE (*idiotically, as he crosses* C.). It's smoking again.

MRS. ROBERTS (*turning and speaking with immense irony*). Do you know, I believe it is. (*With gusto.*) Smoking ! You can't see across that little bit of a room for smoke.

(LAWRENCE *crosses* L., *takes off his hat and coat and hangs them on the stand up* L.)

(*Going to the cupboard down* R. *for a mop.*) If I've told 'em once, I've told 'em fifty times. There's something wrong with that chimney. The place's full o' soot. I give it up.

(LAWRENCE *from now on is getting on with his first duties. He puts the letters on various desks. He fills all the inkwells from a large bottle of ink on the desk at back, puts clean sheets of blotting-paper on the various desks, takes the covers off the two typewriters, and so forth.*)

LAWRENCE (*distributing the letters*). Well, it doesn't matter.

MRS. ROBERTS. It doesn't matter to me if it doesn't matter to them.

LAWRENCE. Mr. Murrison's still away, and Mr. Cornelius won't mind. He nearly always stays out here, anyhow.

MRS. ROBERTS. Good luck to him!

LAWRENCE. Only we'd better get his table out.

MRS. ROBERTS. Come on, then. I want to finish up.

(*They go into the private office and return carrying a small working table. The top is covered with newspapers. They put this near the door into the private office, and then, while* MRS. ROBERTS *is taking off the newspapers and beginning to dust a little,* LAWRENCE *returns to bring out a chair, which he puts behind the table. He then shuts the door. During the dialogue that follows, while* LAWRENCE *gets on with his ink and blotting-paper business,* MRS. ROBERTS *does a little more perfunctory dusting.*)

LAWRENCE (*grumbling, as he goes to* MISS PORRIN'S *desk with ink*). Look at me. Still doing this!

MRS. ROBERTS. Well, what about it?

LAWRENCE. This is an office boy's job.

MRS. ROBERTS. What of it? Aren't you the office boy?

LAWRENCE. Yes.

MRS. ROBERTS. Well, then?

LAWRENCE. I'm nineteen.

MRS. ROBERTS. Never! (*She then stares at him speculatively.*) No, I dare say you are.

LAWRENCE. There's no *dare say* about it. I know I am. I'm nineteen, I've been here nearly five years, and I'm still the office boy.

MRS. ROBERTS (*moving up to* BIDDLE'S *desk*). Fancy!

LAWRENCE. They won't get a kid to do this. They won't promote me. And I'm nineteen. It's absolutely rotten.

MRS. ROBERTS. Why don't you leave, then?

LAWRENCE (*moving across to* BIDDLE'S *desk*). I would if I could get another job. I keep trying.

MRS. ROBERTS (*crossing to mop under* JUDY'S *desk*). That's right. You keep on trying. And if at first you don't succeed—suck eggs. (*She gives a sudden roar of laughter.*)

LAWRENCE (*properly ignoring this and going to* CORNELIUS'S *table down* R.). I've written for hundreds of jobs. I'm taking a correspondence course in wireless now.

MRS. ROBERTS. Now that's a good job—wireless. I've a nephew—my sister's oldest—who's in that. Has a shop of his own in Hackney. Wireless and gramophones.

LAWRENCE. I'm making a gramophone. I've nearly finished it.

Mrs. Roberts. Well, I call that clever. I wouldn't know how to start.

Lawrence. I've made lots of wireless sets.

Mrs. Roberts. You're just like my nephew—the one at Hackney. Of course he's older. But I expect you'll be taking the girls to the pictures now—eh? Or don't you bother with 'em?

Lawrence (*gloomily*). Not much.

Mrs. Roberts. Alfred—my nephew—was just the same. He'd rather be doing his wireless and what not. (*She returns to table* R. *to put down duster and mop.*) But then one fine day—before you could say Jack Robinson—lo and behold!—he goes and gets married, and to as flighty a little piece as ever I saw. One o' these fancy blondes that's always having their hair waved. Goes right from Hackney to Kensington High Street—Pontings and Derry and Toms—to do her shopping. At least, that's what *she* says. (*She empties* Biddle's *waste-paper basket into the pail* C.) I wouldn't trust her a yard. I'd like to have a look at her Derry and Toms. And I think that'll do.

(*She takes her apron off.* Miss Porrin *enters* L. *She is a little woman in her early thirties, spectacled, rather dried up, very simple in manner.*)

Miss Porrin. Oh—good morning, Mrs. Roberts.

Mrs. Roberts. Morning, miss. Quite strangers, aren't we? How are you getting on among it all?

Miss Porrin. Quite well, thank you. And how are you?

Mrs. Roberts (*at the cupboard down* R.). Fair—just fair. (*Putting the things away.*) I'm not getting any thinner and you're not getting any fatter—that's right, isn't it?

Miss Porrin (*taking off her hat and coat*). It looks like it, doesn't it? Good morning, Lawrence.

Lawrence. Good morning.

Mrs. Roberts (*crossing* L. *with the heap of coal*). Here—how's Mr. Cornelius these days?

Miss Porrin. All right, I think.

Mrs. Roberts. He hasn't got married again, has he? (*She puts the coal on the window-sill.*)

Miss Porrin. Oh—dear no. (*She crosses and sits at her desk.*)

Mrs. Roberts. Well, he ought to, a big fine man like him. He must have been a widower now—oh—for seven or eight years. I call it too long. You ought to set about him yourself, Miss Porrin. (*She puts on her coat.*)

Miss Porrin (*brightly*). Such a strange thing happened to me—just now—in the bus. I was carrying my German book—I'm studying German, you know, Mrs. Roberts—I'd been reading it in the bus, but then I'd stopped because it made my eyes ache and the bus gave a jerk and I dropped my German book, and a gentleman sitting opposite picked it up and handed it to me. And do you know—wasn't it strange ?—he was a German himself. He told me so when he saw what the book was. Wasn't it strange ?

MRS. ROBERTS. When are you meeting him ?

MISS PORRIN. Oh, no, certainly not. I'm not meeting him anywhere. It wasn't like that at all. He just picked up the book and——

LAWRENCE (*brutally*). And gave it back to you and told you he was a German. We know.

MISS PORRIN. Don't be rude, please, Lawrence. (*Smiling at* MRS. ROBERTS.) But that's all that happened.

MRS. ROBERTS (*crossing* C. *for the pail and back again*). Good job too, if you ask me. Don't you start taking up with foreigners, Miss Porrin. You don't know where they'll land you.

LAWRENCE (*in melodramatic tone*). White Slave Traffic !

MRS. ROBERTS (*lighting a cigarette*). Well, a girl I used to know married one o' them Germans—a waiter he was—and she got White Slave Traffic all right, a basin full, for he kept her at it, washing and scrubbing and cooking, from morning till night. (*Picking up coal from window-sill.*) Well, I'll be off. And tell 'em they can't blame me for the soot and mess, not till they got that chimney in there properly done. I can't work miracles. If I could, I wouldn't be here. Ta-ta.

(*She goes out.* MISS PORRIN, *at her desk, takes some papers out of a drawer, looks at her typewriter, etc.* LAWRENCE *is slowly finishing his little jobs. The telephone rings.*)

LAWRENCE (*at the telephone*). Hello ! This is Briggs and Murrison. No, we're not. Well, I ought to know, oughtn't I ? We're Briggs (*deliberately*) and Murrison. (*He puts down the receiver.*) And that's silly, when you come to think of it.

MISS PORRIN. What is ? Wrong number ?

LAWRENCE. No. (*He begins sharpening a pencil from* BIDDLE'S *desk into the waste-paper basket* L. *of the desk.*) But every day except Sunday for years at that telephone, I've been saying Briggs and Murrison, Briggs and Murrison, and for years and years you've been writing down Briggs and Murrison, Briggs and Murrison, and all the time there hasn't been a Briggs in the firm at all, only Mr. Murrison——

MISS PORRIN. And Mr. Cornelius. He's a partner.

LAWRENCE. Yes, but I call it a waste of time and breath going on year after year, saying Briggs, writing down Briggs, when there isn't a Briggs. And nearly everybody else doing the same thing.

MISS PORRIN. It doesn't matter.

LAWRENCE. It does. I call it silly and clumsy. You couldn't make a gramophone or a wireless set like that.

MISS PORRIN (*turning to him*). That's because they're new things, Lawrence. All new things are neat, like that, but old things aren't. And a lot of business is really old.

LAWRENCE. Yes, but why? Why shouldn't all this be neat and new and sensible? Why should it be so old-fashioned? I'll bet it needn't be. I'll bet——

(*But* MR. BIDDLE *has entered. He is a clerkly, elderly man, obviously very neat and methodical. He is well wrapped up and carries a folded newspaper—the " Morning Post." He takes off his overcoat, hat, and muffler during the following speeches.*)

BIDDLE. Good morning, Miss Porrin. Good morning, Lawrence.
MISS PORRIN }
LAWRENCE } (*together*). Good morning.

BIDDLE. It s still raw, very raw. Very little sign of spring about. (*He sniffs.*) Hello, has that chimney been smoking again?

LAWRENCE. Yes, Mr. Biddle. Ma Roberts says it's completely blocked up.

BIDDLE (*crossing* R.). We must have it attended to before Mr. Murrison comes back. Mr. Cornelius doesn't mind being out here, but Mr. Murrison wouldn't like it. Where's Miss Evison? (*He unlocks a drawer at his desk.*)

MISS PORRIN. She hasn't come yet.

BIDDLE (*changing his coat*). I shall really have to talk very seriously to Miss Evison. She's late nearly every morning now, and even when she is here, her mind's not on her work.

MISS PORRIN. I don't think she's very well, Mr. Biddle.

BIDDLE. Possibly not, possibly not. But that's no real excuse. Mr. Murrison—in my opinion—isn't very well, hasn't been well for some time, but there he is—in the Midlands—up North—travelling all the time, visiting all our customers, not sparing himself. (*He sits at his desk.*)

(MISS PORRIN *rises and goes to the key-drawer in* BIDDLE'S *desk. She then unlocks the safe and takes out the stamp-book, bank-book and petty cash.*)

LAWRENCE. I think that's quite different.

BIDDLE (*banteringly—starting to open letters*). Oh—you think that's quite different, do you, Lawrence? And why might it be different?

LAWRENCE. This is Mr. Murrison's own show. It's his firm.

BIDDLE. And it's my firm. And it's your firm.

LAWRENCE (*not too rudely*). No, it isn't. This is simply the place where I come and put out blotting-paper and copy letters for twenty-five bob a week.

BIDDLE. Yes, and you don't always do that very well. Get me the Day Book and the In Ledger.

(LAWRENCE *goes to get the books from the table at back. The telephone rings and is answered by* MISS PORRIN, *who has returned to her desk and is busy checking stamps and cash.*)

If that's Howlett and Company, I'll speak to them. Is it? Right.

(MISS PORRIN *plugs the call through to* BIDDLE'S *desk and he takes the telephone.*)

Yes? Biddle here.

(LAWRENCE *drops the books loudly on the* R. *end of* BIDDLE'S *desk and returns to* R. *stool at back.*)

Oh—is it Mr. Howlett? Yes, Biddle. . . . Yes, Mr. Howlett, I quite understand. We're all in the same boat nowadays, aren't we? . . . (*He laughs.*) That's very good. I must remember that. Now listen, Mr. Howlett. Our Mr. Murrison's away . . . Yes, he's gone himself . . . Back on Wednesday . . . No, Mr. Cornelius isn't here yet . . . Now, now, Mr. Howlett . . . you know us . . . Oh no, Mr. Howlett . . . Hello, hello!

(*It is obvious that Mr. Howlett has rung off prematurely, possibly in a temper. As* BIDDLE *puts down the receiver, he looks very worried. His speech that follows, which he gives as he begins looking through the letters, is more for his own benefit than for his listeners.* LAWRENCE *unplugs the extension and returns to the* R. *stool at back.*)

I've been in business for over forty-seven years, and I can tell you that a day of it now is worse than a month of it in the old days. Upon my word, it's misery trying to do business nowadays. Everybody and everything make it as difficult as possible.

MISS PORRIN (*turning round and holding out a letter*). I know Mr. Biddle, I'm so sorry. (*Rising and going to* BIDDLE *with it.*) What about this Excelsior Transport Company's claim? You asked me to remind you.

BIDDLE (*taking the letter*). I should think so. Disgraceful, I call it. Ask that young fellow—what's his name?—Shefford—to come round at once.

(MISS PORRIN *goes to the telephone.*)

Mr. Cornelius had better take it up with him. He'll deal with that lot. He'll give them something to be going on with.

(*He rises and takes this letter, along with some others, over to* COR-NELIUS'S *table, then returns to his own desk to open some more letters.* MISS PORRIN *begins ringing up, but is not heard.*

CORNELIUS *enters* L., *immediately dominating the scene. He is a well-set-up fellow between forty-five and fifty, outwardly an office man, though not too sedentary in appearance, but with a certain eager, humorous, imaginative way with him that suggests that the youth in him is by no means dead. He wears a heavy overcoat, with several newspapers stuck in the pockets, and a soft felt hat which he removes as he enters. He can be smoking a pipe. He arrives with great gusto.*)

CORNELIUS. Good morning. Good morning.
BIDDLE
MISS PORRIN }(*together*). Good morning, Mr. Cornelius.
LAWRENCE
CORNELIUS (*immediately going over to the letters on his table*). Anything from Mr. Murrison?
BIDDLE. I'm afraid not, Mr. Cornelius.
CORNELIUS (*muttering*). Damned nuisance!
BIDDLE. I'm afraid there's no order come through from Chales either.
CORNELIUS (*gloomily, as he moves* C.). I'm not surprised. As soon as I saw young Chales's face, I knew there wasn't an order in it. There was *no* all over it. All permanently screwed down and hermetically sealed. Marvel to me how he ever gives himself any food and drink.

(LAWRENCE *comes down to take* CORNELIUS'S *coat and hat.*)

Why is my table out here again?
LAWRENCE. It's smoky in there again, Mr. Cornelius.
BIDDLE. We shall have to complain to the landlord about that chimney.
CORNELIUS. That's not so easy. We owe him some money. (*Going to his table.*) Miss Evison.
BIDDLE. She's not here yet.
CORNELIUS (*giving his hat and coat to* LAWRENCE). Then she ought to be.

(LAWRENCE *takes the coat and hat off* R.)

BIDDLE. She's getting very slack, I'm afraid—very slack.
CORNELIUS (*sitting at his table*). Not ill, by any chance, is she?
MISS PORRIN. I think she is, Mr. Cornelius.

(BIDDLE *rises and comes down to* L. *of* CORNELIUS'S *table.* CORNELIUS *begins to look through letters and papers in the basket on his table.* LAWRENCE *re-enters and goes back to his stool.*)

CORNELIUS (*as he goes through letters, etc.*). Hm! Solicitor's letter. Cattermole, MacIvor and Pritchet—all very grand, eh?—authorized by something-or-other *Française*—to represent French clients—settlement of claims immediately on best possible terms—that's a nasty one, Biddle.
BIDDLE. It's no use, sir. We shall have to meet them.
CORNELIUS. Looks like it. Small cheque from Shaw and Johnston. Not much, but better than nothing. (*He hands it over.*) Pay it in this morning, and make it look a lot. That'll keep the bank amused until lunch-time.
BIDDLE (*doubtfully*). Shall I take it round myself?
CORNELIUS. Better not. They'll never let you go until we've

agreed to see them all on Wednesday. Send Lawrence round with it.

(BIDDLE *takes the cheque to his desk and endorses it, etc., all very carefully.*)

What's this ? Excelsior Transport Company ? Here, I want to talk to these scoundrels. What have you done, Miss Porrin ?

MISS PORRIN (*crossing to* CORNELIUS). I've rung them up and asked that young man who came here first—you remember him, Mr. Cornelius ?

CORNELIUS. Yes, of course I do. Soapy young twister ! What's his name ?

MISS PORRIN. Shefford—Eric Shefford. I've asked him to come round at once and see you.

CORNELIUS. Quite right. (*He goes through more letters.*)

(MISS PORRIN *goes back to her desk.*)

BIDDLE (*handing an envelope*). Take this round to the bank, Lawrence.

(LAWRENCE *comes down to* BIDDLE, *takes the letter, then collects his hat and goes out* L.)

CORNELIUS. Another grim letter from Czecho-Slovakia—Hecht and Drapok. Why don't they use a typewriter ? And why the devil isn't Miss Evison here ? And if she can't come, why doesn't she let us know ? (*Puzzling over the letter.*) Something about their Dr. Schweig. Oh, what a letter ! These people ought to be in the secret service. (*He puzzles over it.*)

(*There enters* L., *breezily, a fellow with a red face and a hoarse voice and a confidential but loud manner. He is carrying two rugs over his arm. He pauses at the entrance until the word* " Dock," *then crosses* C.)

RUG MAN. Now, I'm a sailor, gentlemen, just landed at Tilbury Dock, and while I was away I picked up a few things that I think would interest you gentlemen——

CORNELIUS (*looking up*). Go away. You're not a sailor. And we don't want any rugs this morning.

RUG MAN. That's right, sir, it's a few rugs I'm selling. (*Going up to* CORNELIUS *and unrolling one.*) Now just cast your eyes over this one——

CORNELIUS (*ferociously*). If that flea-bitten rug isn't out of here in two seconds, I'll throw it out of the window.

RUG MAN (*folding up the rug as he backs* L.—*pugnaciously*). All right, all right.

CORNELIUS (*getting up, dangerously quiet in manner*). It isn't all right.

(*As he steps round the table, the* RUG MAN *suddenly bolts.* CORNELIUS *laughs and crosses to* C. *slowly. The telephone bell rings.* MISS PORRIN *answers it.*)

MISS PORRIN. It's the bank. The manager would like you or Mr. Biddle to call and see him, this morning.

(CORNELIUS *and* BIDDLE *look at each other, rather ominously.*)

CORNELIUS (*crossing* R. *in front of* BIDDLE'S *desk*). You'd better go, Biddle.

(BIDDLE *rises, crosses* L. *and starts putting on his coat.*)

I couldn't get Murrison back before Wednesday afternoon—if they insist upon a meeting as early as possible. And say there's no point in our creditors meeting before Murrison does come back, simply because we're hoping this trip will have saved the situation. (*To* MISS PORRIN.) Tell them Mr. Biddle's coming round at once. (*He returns to examining letters and papers above his table.*) Good God!—what's this. North London Crematorium?

BIDDLE (*crossing* R. *to* CORNELIUS). Oh—I'm sorry, Mr. Cornelius. Those two letters are mine.

(MISS PORRIN *returns the stamp-book and petty cash to the safe.*)

CORNELIUS. Is there another one? Oh—yes. Valley of Rest Crematorium. Here you are. (*Handing them over.*) But why?

BIDDLE (*as he takes the letters, carefully folding them, etc.*). I made up my mind some time ago that I'd like to be cremated, and so I've been getting estimates. There's a difference of about thirty-seven shillings between the two.

CORNELIUS. But perhaps the more expensive people make a better job of it?

BIDDLE (*seriously*). No, I don't think so. Both of them follow the same routine, I believe.

CORNELIUS. Don't tell me what it is.

(BIDDLE *starts to cross* L., *but is held up by the last part of* CORNELIUS'S *speech.*)

Tell them at the bank.

(BIDDLE *goes out, but immediately returns.*)

BIDDLE. Shefford's here—the young man from the Excelsior Transport Company.

CORNELIUS (*grimly*). Tell him to walk straight in.

(BIDDLE *withdraws and* SHEFFORD *enters. He is rather a weedy, vaguely handsome young man, smartly dressed. He is not feeling very comfortable.* MISS PORRIN *is now back at her desk.*)

SHEFFORD. Oh—good morning. Excelsior Transport Company.

You wanted to see me, I think. (*He stops just inside the door, then moves* C.)

CORNELIUS (*taking up paper and moving towards him*). I did. I do.

(SHEFFORD *advances*.)

We've got a claim here from your Company for eight shillings a ton more than we agreed to pay you.

SHEFFORD. No, that's a mistake, I'm afraid.

CORNELIUS. Oh—you mean your people aren't going to claim the extra eight shillings a ton ?

SHEFFORD. No, that's the usual rate. I mean, you must have misunderstood my quotation.

(MISS PORRIN *goes up to back desk, gets ledger and sits on* L. *stool*.)

What I gave you was the actual freight, without clearing and cartage charges, and—er—as you must have seen—it's on all our memo forms—there's an extra twelve and a half per cent for clearing and cartage charges—which works out at an extra eight shillings a ton. It's—er—all perfectly straightforward.

(*There is a pause*.)

CORNELIUS. It's about as straightforward as a corkscrew. You knew very well when we accepted your quotation that we knew nothing about that extra eight shillings a ton, that we were in a hurry to get the metal delivered, and that you were getting the business under false pretences.

SHEFFORD. No, I didn't. How should I know——

CORNELIUS (*going up to* SHEFFORD, *who backs to* L.C.). Because you made a great point of the fact that your quotation was lower than anybody else's, whereas with this extra twelve and a half per cent, it isn't. And if you want to know what I think you are, I'll tell you. You're a young twister. You wanted the business and you didn't care a damn how you got it. Look—(*he tears up the paper and tosses the pieces into* SHEFFORD'S *hat*) that's what we think about you and the Excelsior Transport Company. Now go back and tell them so.

SHEFFORD (*half menacingly*). All right, I will.

(CORNELIUS *turns his back on* SHEFFORD, *who picks the pieces out of his hat, throws them on the floor and goes out*. CORNELIUS *strolls* R., *picks up index cards from his desk and returns to below* MISS PORRIN'S *desk*.)

CORNELIUS. Lot of young men like that about, Miss Porrin. Twisters. If you have it out with some of them, they tell you it's not their fault, it's the system. God knows I don't admire the system. If there is one, it's getting me down. But they'd still be twisting under any system. They couldn't go straight on a desert island.

Miss Porrin (*turning over the pages of a ledger noisily*). I'm afraid that's true. I'm so sorry, Mr. Cornelius.

Cornelius (*with rough good humour*). Well, nobody's blaming it on you, Miss Porrin.

(*A* Little Man *has just sidled quietly in, holding a large bag.*)

Hello, how did you get in?

Little Man (*with insinuating voice*). Good morning, sir, I won't keep you one minute. Now you people have to wash here. You have to provide yourself with towels. Those towels have to be sent to the laundry. They have to be renewed.

Cornelius. Nothing this morning, thank you.

Little Man. Sometimes people use the wrong towels. It's all very dangerous and very expensive. Now I have here a selection of paper towels—as used by some of the biggest firms in the City. They're perfectly efficient, hygienic, and inexpensive——

Cornelius (*firmly*). Not this morning.

Little Man. Just take a look at some of these——

Cornelius. Will you go away?

Little Man (*with a certain pathetic dignity*). I'm sorry. Good morning.

(*He goes out as quietly as he came, drooping a little under the weight of his bag.*)

Cornelius (*irritably*). Where's Lawrence? Why isn't he here to keep those fellows out? Either they're blustering and then they make you angry, or they're pathetic—like that poor little devil—and then they make you feel miserable. (*He returns to his desk.*) And all the time there are a thousand things to be thinking about. And what on earth's become of Miss Evison? Is she on the telephone at home?

Miss Porrin (*rising*). No, I don't think so, Mr. Cornelius. (*Coming down* C.) And I do agree with you about those men who come round with things. There seem to be more and more of them.

Cornelius. There are. We'll all be doing it soon. All calling on one another with rugs and paper towels and shaving-soap.

(Lawrence *enters.* Miss Porrin *goes back to* L. *stool.*)

Lawrence, open that " Enquiries " window of yours, ask 'em what they want, and don't let 'em in unless they've got some proper business here.

(Lawrence *opens the enquiries window, which is in the wall just upstage of the telephone switchboard. Meanwhile, the telephone rings.* Miss Porrin *answers it.*)

If you don't want to have to get rid of a corpse about lunch time, Lawrence, then don't let any more of these fellows in.

(Lawrence *goes up to* R. *stool at back and sits.*)

Miss Porrin. It's Brandings, of Birmingham. They want to speak to you or Mr. Murrison.

Cornelius (*happily*). That's more like it. (*He rises and goes to the telephone.*) Hello! Brandings? Cornelius speaking . . . Oh, yes—is that Mr. Flockton? Thought I recognized your voice . . . Yes, of course. Much as you like. That's what we're here for, as the parson said to . . . Yes, exactly same quality as before. Our people over there are very dependable . . . How much? My dear fellow, you're joking. We couldn't buy it at anything like that figure, not with the pound only worth twelve and sixpence over there. . . . No, but we can't help it either. Now, be reasonable, Mr. Flockton. We can quote you—— Hello, hello! (*He lets the receiver drop.*)

(Lawrence *crosses and unplugs the 'phone.*)

Miss Porrin. Shall I get them again?

Cornelius (*bitterly*). No, he meant to go. (*Returning and sitting at his desk.*) They don't even wait to say good-bye now. They just ring off. They've no use for you. You're out.

(*There is a knock on the door.* Lawrence *crosses* L.)

It must be taking Murrison all his time to collect a few more orders. I don't know how he's doing it—if he is doing it.

Lawrence (*through the little window*). Name, please? What name? (*To* Cornelius.) Mr. Coleman. He says it's important.

Cornelius (*getting up*). Yes, yes, of course. I want to see him.

(Lawrence *admits* Coleman, *a middle-aged business man with a sharp jerky manner.* Cornelius *crosses* c. *and meets* Coleman, *who comes* c. *from door.*)

Morning, Mr. Coleman.

Coleman. Morning, Mr. Cornelius.

(Lawrence *goes back to* R. *stool.*)

Cornelius. How's copper wire these days?

Coleman (*grimly*). You know. (*He produces a piece of paper, confidentially.*) Heard anything from Canada lately?

Cornelius. Not for a fortnight. Have you?

Coleman. Yes. And I was passing, so thought I'd slip in and tell you.

Cornelius. Very good of you, my dear chap.

Coleman. We had a night-letter cable from our man Blake in Ottawa. Just came this morning. Here. (*They look at it.*) You see? Embargo's certain now on everything but low-grade sheet metal.

Cornelius. Yes. (*Grimly.*) I like that last bit. All the best and he's just going fishing. What do we reply to that? All the worst and we're just going to cut our throats, eh?

Act I.] CORNELIUS.

COLEMAN. Make a difference to you people too, won't it?

CORNELIUS. Yes. We haven't been buying much from Canada lately, or it would make a lot of difference. As it is, it takes the last crumb of cheese and leaves us in the mouse-trap.

COLEMAN. It's a great life, isn't it?

CORNELIUS (*solemnly*). "And we are glad to report that business conditions everywhere are improving." Loud cheers from everybody present, all living on gilt-edged securities.

COLEMAN (*with slight laugh*). Well, thought you'd like to have the news. (*He makes towards the door.*)

CORNELIUS. Much obliged to you, Mr. Coleman.

(BIDDLE *enters, looking rather miserable.*)

COLEMAN (*going*). Not at all. 'Morning.

(*He nods to* BIDDLE *as he goes out.* BIDDLE *says,* "Good morning.")

CORNELIUS (*crossing* R. *and sitting at his table*). We're cut off from Canada now, Biddle. Shan't be able to buy a pound of decent metal there. I notice you don't look very cheerful. (*He lights his pipe.*)

BIDDLE (*with small forced smile*). Don't I, sir? I'm sorry. I'm afraid I wasn't feeling very cheerful. (*He begins taking his things off.*)

CORNELIUS. What happened?

BIDDLE (*crossing* R. *to* CORNELIUS). Well, as you know, Mr. Cornelius, I've been going round to the Middlesex and Central Bank a good long time now. I knew most of the old lot very well. I used to like going round there, sir. I regarded it as one of the pleasantest parts of my duty. We used to have a good deal of quiet fun——

CORNELIUS (*pleasantly sardonic*). It must have been very quiet.

BIDDLE. Well, you know—Mr. Cornelius—we'd chaff one another, have our little jokes.

CORNELIUS. And there aren't any more little jokes, eh?

BIDDLE. Well, it's a bit of a shock to go in as I did this morning —the manager was quite pleasant, but——

CORNELIUS (*lowering voice*). What happened?

BIDDLE (*coming nearer, confidentially*). They're pressing very hard. They say it's head office.

CORNELIUS. You told them about Murrison making a big drive for orders?

BIDDLE. I made a great deal of it, said you staked everything on it.

CORNELIUS. I do. I know Bob Murrison. He can do it.

BIDDLE. I had to promise we'd make a definite statement to them and the other creditors here on Wednesday afternoon.

CORNELIUS (*rising*). I thought you'd have to.

(*There is a pause.*)

B

(*He moves round above the table.*) Well, I'll wire Mr. Murrison at once. And you'd better let all these people know—these solicitors—Cattermole, MacIvor and the rest of it. And the Central Forwarding Company.

(BIDDLE *goes to his desk.*)

And—Miss Porrin—you'd better wire Hecht and Drapok——

(MISS PORRIN *comes down* R.C. *from back.*)

I don't know where their Dr. Schweig is—telling 'em we're having a meeting of creditors—an *informal* meeting of creditors—(*he sits*) here on Wednesday afternoon, about three.

MISS PORRIN. Yes, Mr. Cornelius. Hecht and Drapok. (*She goes up to the 'phone.*)

CORNELIUS. Those are your men, Biddle. (*He hands him some letters.*) And cheer up. A lot of things can happen on Wednesday.

(CORNELIUS *begins writing furiously.* BIDDLE *looks thoughtfully at the letters in his hand, then walks slowly up to his desk with them and sits.* MISS PORRIN *is listening at the telephone. She puts it down in disgust.*)

MISS PORRIN. Can I send Lawrence down to the post office with this telegram to Hecht and Drapok? I can't get through to foreign telegrams on the telephone.

CORNELIUS (*still writing quickly*). Yes, and he can take this one to Mr. Murrison with him, too.

(LAWRENCE *comes down and stands by* CORNELIUS *while he finishes.* MISS PORRIN *crosses* R. *and gets money from the cash-box in the safe. She then comes down and meets* LAWRENCE C., *giving him the money and her telegraph form.* LAWRENCE *hurries out* L. CORNELIUS *relaxes.*)

By the way, there's the landlord. He ought to be told about Wednesday. That old boy's treated us very decently, hasn't he?

BIDDLE. Very decently indeed, sir. We can't complain at all in that direction.

MISS PORRIN (C.). May I say something, Mr. Cornelius?

CORNELIUS. Why not?

(BIDDLE, *who has a large ledger open, looks up.*)

MISS PORRIN (*with timid resolution*). Well, I think—when you take everything into consideration—that a lot of people are very good. (*She gives a quick nervous laugh and returns to her work at* L. *stool.*)

CORNELIUS. Perhaps. But you've got to take a devil of a lot into consideration, though. It seems to me sometimes——

(*He stops and stares, because a young woman, cheaply but fairly smartly dressed, and with a very assured manner, has just entered the office. She is carrying a small case.*)

YOUNG WOMAN (*brightly*). Good morning.
CORNELIUS (*rising*). Good morning.
YOUNG WOMAN (*crossing* C.). I'm sure you gentlemen are needing some shaving-soap, tooth-paste, talcum powder, brilliantine——
CORNELIUS. I'm not. Are you, Biddle?
BIDDLE (*looking up*). Oh—no, certainly not. (*He returns to his ledger.*)
YOUNG WOMAN (*opening her case and crossing to* CORNELIUS *with a terrific smile*). Now, I'm sure I can tempt you.
CORNELIUS. I'm sure you can, too.
YOUNG WOMAN. Well then? All good new lines. Cheaper than the shops. What about some shaving-soap, then?
MISS PORRIN (*suddenly and surprisingly coming forward*). Please —go away. Go away at once. Nobody wants anything here. And you know very well they don't.
YOUNG WOMAN (*surprised*). Here, wait a minute. I wasn't talking to you.
MISS PORRIN (*indignantly*). I know. But I don't care. It's disgraceful—taking advantage—just because you're a woman. You're much worse than the men.

(*The telephone rings.*)

CORNELIUS (*rather dryly*). Telephone, Miss Porrin.

(MISS PORRIN, *with a final glare at the intruder, turns to answer the telephone. The* YOUNG WOMAN *turns her batteries on* CORNELIUS *again.*)

(*Mumbling.*) All right. I'll have a tube of shaving-cream. That'll do. How much?
YOUNG WOMAN. Two shillings, please.
CORNELIUS (*producing the money*). Cheaper than the shops, eh? I wonder what shops. Here you are. (*He takes the shaving-cream and hands over the money.*)
YOUNG WOMAN. Nothing else? Thank you. Good morning. (*To* MISS PORRIN.) Good morning.

(*She goes out.*)

MISS PORRIN (*rather severely*). It's Mr. Howlett, wishing to speak to you, Mr. Cornelius.
CORNELIUS (*sitting at his table*). Tell him I'm out, Biddle, but that I'm writing to him.

(BIDDLE *rises, goes to the telephone and can repeat this message while* MISS PORRIN *is talking as below.* MISS PORRIN *crosses to above the table with a letter.*)

Miss Porrin. What about this account, Mr. Cornelius? (*She hands it to him.*)
Cornelius (*looking at it*). Eighty-seven pounds! I didn't know it was as much as that.
Miss Porrin. It's been owing several months, and there was the typewriter and the table and chair, as well as the usual things.
Cornelius. Well, we can't pay it, that's all. Are they pressing us hard?
Miss Porrin. I'm afraid they are.

(Biddle *returns to his desk and sits.*)

Cornelius. I could talk to them—but it doesn't look very good when——
Miss Porrin. If you like, I think I could go and talk to them. They know me, because I've always ordered the things there. I could tell them you're both away and that one of you has to pass the account before we can settle it.
Cornelius. Yes, all right. Try that. Go round now.

(Miss Porrin *starts to cross* L. *and is held up* C.)

(*Handing her the account back.*) I say, you were very severe with that young woman who came in just now, weren't you?
Miss Porrin (*hesitating, then gathering courage*). Well—Mr. Cornelius—you don't mind my saying this, do you? But I do think it's such a shame—you're so firm with all those poor men who come round worrying us, and then, just because this is a girl and she comes in so impudently—oh, they're so much worse than the men. I'm sorry for most of the men, but these women—they're horrible. (*She goes for her hat and coat.*)
Cornelius (*ruefully*). I dare say you're right.
Miss Porrin. I—I know I am. They're just vulgar—vulgar—shameless——
Cornelius (*humorously*). Steady. Steady now.
Miss Porrin (*rather triumphantly*). Sirens!

(*And she makes quite a triumphant exit.*)

Cornelius. And that's that, Biddle.
Biddle (*thoughtfully*). I've noticed before, sir—and you must have done, too—the female sex hasn't a lot of sympathy for itself.
Cornelius (*rising*). I have noticed it. (*He crosses slowly below the table to* L.C. *and sits on the edge of* Miss Porrin's *desk.*) And how the quiet little shy ones hate the big bouncing ones.

(*He takes up the bank book and begins making little calculations on paper from it. He looks thoughtfully across at* Biddle, *who is still dealing with the ledger.*)

Biddle, suppose we can't carry on. What's going to happen to you?
Biddle (*slowly*). Well, it might be worse, sir. It might be a

lot worse, sir. I've a married daughter living in South Devon. They've a little business, and they'd like us to join them. We've got something saved up. We've been careful——

CORNELIUS (*dryly*). You must have been.

BIDDLE. Yes, we've been very careful, and so we've got something saved up. And that would come in useful down in South Devon. And it's very nice down there—very nice indeed.

CORNELIUS. That's good. But don't you ever feel—doesn't it ever come over you quite suddenly—that you've been wasting your time?

BIDDLE (*seriously*). But I don't waste my time, Mr. Cornelius.

CORNELIUS. I don't mean that. I mean, that you've wasted your life, just as if you'd taken it and poured it down a drain.

BIDDLE. No, I never think that for a minute. I've led an honest and useful life, Mr. Cornelius, and I'm not ashamed of it and I don't regret any of it.

CORNELIUS. Well, that's something to be thankful for. It would be horrible, at your age, if you felt anything else. It's bad enough at my age. You're a lucky man, Biddle.

BIDDLE. Yes, Mr. Cornelius, in some ways I am. I've always been able to work, and I've always enjoyed my work. The fact is, Mr. Cornelius, there's always been something very attractive to me about figures, numbers. In a sort of way, they're alive. For instance, seven has got quite a different character from eight. And five is one sort of person and six is quite a different sort of person. Like all of us.

CORNELIUS (*amused*). So all the time, while you were pretending to work, you've been having the most astonishing adventures in that corner?

BIDDLE. In a way—yes, I have.

CORNELIUS. I tell you—you're a lucky man, Biddle. (*He rises and crosses to* BIDDLE.) You've never felt you were worrying the hair off your head; the sight out of your eyes, for what was nothing better than a piece of damned futility. I have—sometimes. Only sometimes. If I hadn't been working here with Bob Murrison——

(*He stares at nothing for a moment, then turns back to his accounts. A man in his early thirties enters, carrying a sample case. He still holds himself well, but he looks pale, thin, nervous. He wears a short moustache and has the rather clipped speech of the ex-officer.* CORNELIUS *returns to his table and sits.*)

EX-OFFICER (*not very confidently—standing* L. *below the door*). Good morning, gentlemen. I'd like to show you some samples of the stationery and other office supplies my firm is offering.

CORNELIUS (*shortly*). No, thanks. 'Morning.

EX-OFFICER. Any kind of stationery, carbons, typewriter ribbons——

CORNELIUS (*decisively*). No.

Ex-Officer (*sticking it*). I'm sure you will find we can quote you office supplies at a very cheap rate. And they're all—er—of first-class quality. My firm——

Cornelius. We don't want anything, and I don't want to hear about your firm.

Ex-Officer (*desperately, coming down* c.). Can't I possibly interest you, sir, in our office stationery, carbons, ribbons——

Cornelius (*jumping up*). You're just being a nuisance, wasting our time as well as your own. (*Crossing* c.) There's a cupboard full of stationery, carbons—(*in his impatience he takes the* Ex-Officer *by the shoulder and swings him towards the cupboard down* R.) ribbons, paper fasteners, rubbers, and God knows what. More than we can use up this year. Stacks of it, stacks of it. Look! Here, what's the matter? (*For the* Ex-Officer *is in danger of collapsing.*) Steady, man. (*Supporting him.*) What's the matter? Here, sit down, sit down.

(Biddle *rises, crosses* L.C. *and turns* Miss Porrin's *chair to face front. The* Ex-Officer *sits.* Biddle *stands behind the chair and* Cornelius R. *of it. The* Ex-Officer *closes his eyes for a moment, then, with an effort, opens them.*)

Ex-Officer (*with an effort*). Sorry. Suddenly felt giddy.

(Biddle *crosses to the window* L. *and opens it.*)

Did a stupid thing—this morning. Only had a cup of coffee before coming out. Not enough perhaps on a cold morning.

Cornelius (*staring hard at his face*). No, not enough. And you hadn't enough yesterday or the day before either. In fact, you're half-starved, aren't you? That's why you nearly collapsed.

Ex-Officer (*rather confusedly*). Have been a bit on short rations lately. But—anyhow—feeling rather—cheap.

Cornelius (*irritably*). You can't come in here starving like that, trying to sell us things we don't want. What are we to do?

Ex-Officer. All right. I'm going.

Cornelius. No you're not, not for a minute or two. But why do you do it? Why don't you get something else to do?

Ex-Officer (*grimly*). What?

Cornelius. Well, what were you originally?

Ex-Officer. Air Force.

Cornelius. Officer?

Ex-Officer. Yes. Had a bad breakdown. North-West Frontier. Then I was broke.

Cornelius. But surely you could have done something better than trying to sell that stuff? I know jobs are hard to get. But why stick to England at all? Why didn't you go to one of the colonies or to South America?

Ex-Officer. No money. I tried. They don't want you any more in those places unless you've got capital. They don't want you anywhere. My God—you don't think I didn't try everything before doing this?

CORNELIUS (*incredulous—not contradicting*). I can't believe the world's all shut up like that—with a *Keep Out* sign everywhere.

EX-OFFICER. That's what it looked like to me. You haven't—a cigarette, by any chance?

(CORNELIUS *feels for one, then looks at* BIDDLE. BIDDLE *gives the* EX-OFFICER *a cigarette and* CORNELIUS *lights it.*)

Thanks. I take it—you wouldn't like any stationery or ribbons or anything?

(CORNELIUS *goes* R. *and slams the cupboard door shut.*)

Sorry to be offensive, but a chap's got to live. Or at least, I suppose so. No carbons? No account books?

CORNELIUS (*crossing to* C. *again*). Look here, if I spent another penny on that stuff, when we're jammed up with it, I'd be acting dishonestly towards my partner. But I can't see you go out in that condition. You won't be able to carry that case of yours soon. Take this (*he holds out a note*) and for God's sake treat yourself to a good square meal before you do anything else.

EX-OFFICER. Nice of you—but——

CORNELIUS. Oh—take it—(*he forces it on him*) we want to get on with our work.

EX-OFFICER (*rising*). Sorry. No use telling you I'll pay you back some time, I suppose.

(BIDDLE *closes the window.*)

I will though, if I can sell any of this stuff. And I might be able to once I've got some hot food and a drink inside me. (*He picks up his hat and bag.*)

CORNELIUS. I doubt it. For the love of Mike, try to sell something else.

EX-OFFICER. Yes, but what?

CORNELIUS. Well, anything but that. We get scores of fellows with that stuff. Be original. Strike out for yourself. Come round with fresh lobsters or pipe cleaners or dirty postcards. Think of some new way of earning a living. There must be dozens that nobody's ever tried.

EX-OFFICER. No doubt. But don't you see, if I was capable of inventing a new kind of job, I should never have been in this fix at all. I'm not clever enough. Don't pretend to be. What gets me down is that I'm not allowed to earn my living in any of the old ways. (*Indicating the note.*) And thanks again for this. I'll pay you back some day. So long. (*He moves to the door.*)

CORNELIUS. Good luck! (*He watches him go, then turns to* BIDDLE.) D'you think that's true, Biddle—that here's a fellow, willing to work, fairly intelligent, who not only can't get anything to do here—I can understand that—but who finds the whole world closed to him, bolted and barred?

BIDDLE. I'm afraid it might be. (*He returns to his desk and sits.*)

CORNELIUS (*with some agitation*). I can't believe it. If you're willing to work hard, willing to take risks, ready to be scorched or frozen, drowned or sent half-mad with thirst (*he crosses to the window* L. *and looks out*) there must be openings for you somewhere in the world. They can't have closed everything up, so that we're all like bees in a glass case. It's unthinkable, Biddle. I've always had at the back of my mind a little open door, with plantations and jungles and pampas and quartz mountains just outside it—with the sun on 'em. (*Crossing back to his table.*) Don't tell me that all the time that little door's not been open, has been locked from the outside, screwed fast.

BIDDLE. The Coventry people are worrying about that consignment of circles we sent off last week.

CORNELIUS. They've no need to grumble. We're out of pocket now on that deal, thanks to the nice kind French people. Sharks with beards and attaché-cases. (*He sits.*)

(*The telephone rings.* BIDDLE *rises and answers it.*)

BIDDLE (*at the telephone*). Briggs and Murrison . . . Who? Oh . . . I'll see. Just a minute. (*To* CORNELIUS, *covering the mouthpiece.*) It's the Income Tax people—the inspector—wants to speak to you.

CORNELIUS. Oh! New idea, telephoning, isn't it? But I believe I ought to have seen that chap this morning.

BIDDLE. What shall I say?

CORNELIUS (*rising*). I'll talk to him. (*He goes below the table to the telephone on* BIDDLE'S *desk.*) Hello . . .

(BIDDLE *goes to the down stage end of* MISS PORRIN'S *desk.*)

Yes, this is Cornelius . . . Oh, yes. Sorry I didn't turn up . . . Yes, I dare say it is important, but so is this business—to us, and you seem to have an interest in it too. What was it? . . . Well, I'm here at the end of the telephone. What's the matter with that? You don't want to *look* at me, do you, my dear chap? . . . (*He winks at* BIDDLE.) A legacy? Yes, I had. A small one. . . . What did I *do* with it? I spent it. . . . Yes, I spent it. . . . What *on*? My dear sir, you take a most flatteringly deep interest in my affairs, don't you? . . . Well, the Government then. . . . All right, tell the Government I spent it recklessly and luxuriously and with the most devilish abandon. . . . Yes, beautiful mad women.

(BIDDLE *turns round and looks at* CORNELIUS.)

Processions with elephants and brass bands through Oriental cities. A private guard of swordsmen and detectives with machine-guns.

Great glittering white yachts. Fountains of wine. Yes, and tell the Government I've no further interest in the country. I've dissolved the partnership. They can keep what they've already had out of me, but they won't get any more. I'm on my own now. . . . All right then, my dear sir. Send me the pink or buff form and I'll deal with it. Good morning. (*He puts down the telephone and returns to his table and sits.*)

BIDDLE (*chuckling*). I wonder what he's thinking. (*He goes to his desk and sits.*)

CORNELIUS. He's thinking I'm off my head, and he's probably right. This famous legacy he's worrying about—wanting to know what I did with it, mind you—came to me from an old aunt of mine in Waltham Cross, and amounted to exactly eighty-seven pounds and ten shillings. What did I do with it? Tut-t-t-t! (*He tries to work, but there is the sound of voices outside.*)

(*Off stage—noise of* LAWRENCE *saying* " All right, I'll tell him," *etc.*)

Now what's this?

(LAWRENCE *enters and puts his hat on a peg.*)

What is it?

LAWRENCE. It's Miss Evison. (*He stands just inside the door.*)

CORNELIUS. Well, if it's Miss Evison, why doesn't she come in? We've been waiting for her half the morning. What's the matter?

LAWRENCE. It's not *our* Miss Evison, sir. It's her sister.

CORNELIUS. Oh! Well, bring her in, then. She must have a message for us.

(LAWRENCE, R. *of it, holds the door open and* JUDY EVISON *enters. She is a girl about twenty, small, pretty, with an engaging child-like quality that makes her markedly different from anybody else who has appeared on the scene. She is oddly composed in manner. She is cheaply, but quite charmingly dressed.*)

JUDY (*entering to* L.C., *then stopping*). Good morning.
CORNELIUS (*getting up*). Good morning.
JUDY. Are you Mr. Cornelius?
CORNELIUS. Yes.
JUDY (*not impudently*). You're rather different from what I expected.

(LAWRENCE *stands down* L., *above* JUDY'S *desk.*)

CORNELIUS (*good-humouredly*). Well, I don't know that I care much about that. What's happened to your sister?

JUDY. I came to tell you. Her husband's been suddenly taken ill in Newcastle.

CORNELIUS. Her husband! I never knew she had a husband. Did you know that Miss Evison had a husband, Biddle?

(BIDDLE *stares at* JUDY, *then suddenly looks at* CORNELIUS.)

BIDDLE. Not the least idea of it, sir.
JUDY. Well, she has. She was married about six months ago.
CORNELIUS. But why didn't she tell us? I call it very unfriendly of her, getting married and never saying a word about it. Not only unfriendly, but also underhand, deceitful.
JUDY (*smiling*). Not really. I can explain.
CORNELIUS (*coming* C., *above his table, to* JUDY). All right then, explain. But see you make a good job of it, because we're resentful —aren't we, Biddle?

(JUDY *begins laughing*.)

What are you giggling about? There's nothing to giggle about.
JUDY (*still laughing a little*). I'm sorry. But—I think you're funny. My sister—used to talk about you, and I always thought you sounded funny——
CORNELIUS (*humorously exasperated*). But my dear young woman, you can't come here—calmly announcing that your sister's married, then giggling, then telling me to my face that I'm funny.

(LAWRENCE *suddenly explodes with laughter, takes out his handkerchief and drops screws and bits of wire, etc.*)

That'll do, Lawrence. Outside.
LAWRENCE (*recovering*). But where to, sir?
CORNELIUS. Anywhere. Haven't you something for him to do, Biddle? (*He turns up to* BIDDLE.)
BIDDLE. Take this round to the Central Forwarding people, Lawrence.

(LAWRENCE *goes to* BIDDLE, *takes the letter, and pauses on his way out to look at* JUDY. *He then picks up his hat and giggles again before going off.*)

JUDY (*calmly*). I'm sorry. I didn't realize that boy was so silly.
CORNELIUS (*down* C., *to* JUDY). You seem to me a very extraordinary young woman. Now tell us about your sister.
JUDY. They hadn't much money when they married. Her husband's a traveller for a firm of chemists—but he's only just begun. And Ann thought that if she told you she was married, she might lose her job here, and they couldn't afford that, and it didn't matter about her working because Alec was away so much. And now he's ill—pneumonia—in Newcastle, and she's rushed up there to be with him. And I think she ought to go, don't you?
CORNELIUS. Yes. (*He crosses up* C. *to* MISS PORRIN'S *desk.*) But I wish she'd told us she had a husband who at any moment might suddenly get pneumonia in Newcastle.
BIDDLE. It's very inconvenient indeed.
JUDY (*crossing in front of* CORNELIUS *to* BIDDLE). Yes, I know. But you see—that's why I'm here.
CORNELIUS. Oh?

JUDY. I'm a shorthand-typist too, and I can do her work quite easily.

CORNELIUS. But why haven't you got a job of your own?

JUDY. I left mine last week.

CORNELIUS. Why? I thought nobody left their jobs nowadays.

JUDY. I do. You see, I was working for a Spaniard—he was a fat yellow sort of man with a black beard—and he'd come to England because he had a theory about pigs——

CORNELIUS. Pigs?

JUDY. Yes, pigs. (*To* CORNELIUS.) And he used to be out all day and I had to stay in a very dirty little room in Victoria with nothing to do, and then he'd come in about five o'clock and begin dictating long long letters—in the queerest English—all about pigs, and then I had to stay there hours and type them. I hated it. (*She turns to* BIDDLE.) He was a very smelly sort of man, too.

CORNELIUS. Perhaps it was the pigs.

JUDY (*seriously, to* CORNELIUS). No, I think it was something he ate. Anyhow, I loathed it. So I left.

CORNELIUS. And now you'd like to come here.

JUDY. Yes, I wouldn't mind it here. (*She crosses* L.) And I'm quite a good shorthand-typist. Better than Ann, as a matter of fact.

CORNELIUS. I dare say, but you see we're used to her and it might take us a long time to get used to you.

JUDY. But she may be away for weeks.

CORNELIUS. That's true. But we could easily get somebody. You seem such a formidable young woman.

JUDY (*demurely*). I'm not. I'm very quiet. (*She smiles at him and finally he grins back.*)

(*There is a pause.*)

CORNELIUS. All right. That's your place over there. (*He indicates the table by the window.*) You'd better start now—er—Miss——

JUDY. My name's Judy. (*She goes down* L., *puts her case by the table, then goes up* L. *and takes off her coat and hat.*)

CORNELIUS. You already know my name. And this is Mr. Biddle, the cashier.

(MISS PORRIN *enters.*)

Oh—and this is Miss Porrin, who'll show you what to do, if necessary.

(MISS PORRIN *stands just inside the door, then takes off her coat.* JUDY *is* L. *of her.*)

(*To* MISS PORRIN, *who is regarding* JUDY *with surprise and some disfavour.*) Miss Porrin, this is Miss Judy Evison, who's come to take her sister's place. (*He turns away.*)

MISS PORRIN. You're—very young, aren't you?

JUDY (*brightly*). Yes, aren't I? But I've had a very good training.

(*She moves down to her desk, sits and examines her machine.* MISS PORRIN *goes to her desk and sits. There is a sharp rap on the door.* CORNELIUS *goes to the enquiries window and takes a telegram. He opens it and reads it, and is plainly puzzled by it.*)

CORNELIUS. I say, Biddle. (*As* BIDDLE *rises and comes forward.*) I've a wire here from Mr. Murrison. Read it. (*As* BIDDLE *reads it.*) I think it must be one of his jokes.

BIDDLE. Funny time this for joking, sir.

CORNELIUS. Yes, it's the only explanation.

(*He comes down* C. BIDDLE *follows him.*)

Why should I know anything about two men following him? It's some old joke of his that he's reviving and that I've forgotten. You see what that means, Biddle?

BIDDLE. No.

CORNELIUS. It means he's in good spirits. Probably got a bagful of new orders that he's keeping as a surprise for us.

BIDDLE (*dubiously*). Well, I hope so, Mr. Cornelius. (*He hands back the telegram and returns to his desk.*)

CORNELIUS (*indicating the telegram*). And this is just like him. (*He goes* R. *and sits at his table.*) Now then, Miss Evison the Second, just bring a notebook and pencil over here, please.

(JUDY *crosses with a notebook, taking up a position just behind him, standing.*)

(*Handing her a letter.*) Those people. "Dear Sirs, In reply to your letter of the eleventh instant, we regret to inform you that no further supplies of the French metal—your number A seventy-three—(*he pauses*)—are—er—available at anything like the price you mention, owing to present foreign exchanges. We—er—should like to draw your attention—however—to our Canadian sheet metal "—too fast?

JUDY. Much.

CORNELIUS (*more slowly*). —" which will not be available er— long at present prices—owing——

(*A voice is heard outside saying,* " Briggs and Murrison? 'Morning," *in the brisk manner of postmen, and now* LAWRENCE *enters with two letters and a parcel. He hands one letter to* BIDDLE *and the other letter and parcel to* CORNELIUS.)

(*To* JUDY.). Just a minute.

(*He opens the letter, which he tosses aside, then opens the parcel, which contains a large octavo modern book. At this moment the telephone rings.* MISS PORRIN *answers it and after a moment can be heard saying, "Mr. Cornelius? Yes, I'll ask him." There is now a sharp rapping at the enquiries window, which* LAWRENCE *opens. He can now be heard saying to the invisible caller, "Mr. Cornelius? What name, please?" Meanwhile,* CORNELIUS, *after looking at the title and title-page of his book, is now glancing at the first page.*)

(*To* JUDY.) I ordered this book from a second-hand catalogue. Don't often do that. It's about the Andes.

MISS PORRIN. Mr. Cornelius, you're wanted on the telephone.

LAWRENCE. Mr. Cornelius, there's somebody called Frensham wants to see you.

JUDY. Mr. Cornelius, what about this letter?

(*These three speeches can overlap.*)

CORNELIUS (*still staring at the book*). I like the look of this. Listen. "After a week in the Indian village, we decided to take the track into the clouds, to find among those heights the lost city of the Incas . . ."

CURTAIN.

ACT II

The Office, Wednesday afternoon.
(*For slight alteration in the setting, see Property Plot.*)

JUDY *is working down* L., *typing letters.* MISS PORRIN *is carefully copying out some figures at her desk at the back. Then* MISS PORRIN *obviously comes to the end of the task, for she closes the office books she has been glancing at, and rises with two sheets of paper in her hand.* JUDY *keeps on typing. As* MISS PORRIN *moves towards the door of the private office, it opens and* CORNELIUS *comes out a step or two. He is holding a half-finished glass of stout in one hand and a half-eaten ham sandwich in the other. He is chewing the sandwich as he comes out.*

MISS PORRIN (*eagerly*). Oh—Mr. Cornelius——
CORNELIUS (*his mouth rather full*). Yes?
MISS PORRIN (*showing papers*). I've got those figures out for you—if you should want them at the meeting this afternoon.
CORNELIUS (*looking at them as she holds the papers out*). Yes, might be very useful—very useful indeed. They're for the last three years, of course?
MISS PORRIN. Yes, they cover everything for the last three years. And you'll find them quite accurate.
CORNELIUS. I'm sure I shall. Thanks very much, Miss Porrin. You ought to be going off and getting some lunch now. You're very late.
MISS PORRIN. Oh—it doesn't matter. I—I never eat much lunch.
CORNELIUS (*thoughtfully*). No, I don't suppose I do—really. I like a better lunch than this though, only to-day I hadn't time to go out and get it. You know, Miss Porrin—— (*He stops and takes a thoughtful bite of sandwich.*)
MISS PORRIN (*hopefully*). Yes, Mr. Cornelius?
CORNELIUS. There's something queer about the ham in this sandwich. I told Lawrence to get it at the pub below. I hope he did. As a rule, a pub makes you a good sandwich—a good, hearty, honest sandwich. But this ham tastes—(*He drops a piece of ham into his mouth.*)—Put those figures down there, please, Miss Porrin—

(MISS PORRIN *puts the papers on* BIDDLE'S *desk.*)

—it tastes—there's a sort of cheesy flavour. Now why should it taste like that?

JUDY (*calmly calling across*). Because it's bad, I expect.
MISS PORRIN (*too sweetly*). Shall I help you to finish those letters, Miss Evison? (*She moves towards* JUDY.)
JUDY. No, thanks, I'm just doing the last.

(CORNELIUS *has now put the last of his sandwich in his mouth, and has taken up the papers* MISS PORRIN *put down and gives them another glance.*)

MISS PORRIN (*eagerly*). Oh—Mr. Cornelius—— (*She crosses* R. *to him.*)
CORNELIUS (*negligently*). Yes?
MISS PORRIN. I do hope everything—everything—you know—goes on all right this afternoon at the meeting.
CORNELIUS. Yes, of course, we all do.
MISS PORRIN. Oh—I don't mean just for the firm and for myself —but for your sake, Mr. Cornelius. I know you've worked so hard and been so worried and yet been so cheerful—and—and bright —and kind to us all—and you do *deserve* everything to be all right.
CORNELIUS (*rather astonished*). Well—yes, I suppose so. I don't know.
MISS PORRIN (*eagerly*). And I appreciate it. I *do* appreciate it, Mr. Cornelius. And if there's anything more I can do, just to help you—I'd love to do it, I really would.

(*She looks beseechingly up at him. He stares at her, rather embarrassed.*)

CORNELIUS. No, thank you, Miss Porrin. There's absolutely nothing else you can do, and you've been very, very helpful. Now go and get some lunch. And don't worry about this meeting. Mr. Murrison will be back and then we'll surprise some of these creditors.
MISS PORRIN (*timidly laying a finger on his arm, then hastily withdrawing it, then smiling and blinking*). Oh—I do hope so. (*She goes quickly for her hat and coat* L. *and puts them on.*)
CORNELIUS. And don't forget you needn't come back until about five. That'll give us time to get the meeting over. (*He wipes his mouth with his handkerchief.*) You needn't come back at all this afternoon——
MISS PORRIN (*with a false brightness*). Yes, of course I will. (*She looks at* JUDY.) There may be lots and lots to do.

(*As she hurries out,* CORNELIUS *takes a last drink of his stout and* JUDY *takes her last letter out of the machine and begins reading it over.*)

CORNELIUS (*almost to himself*). There's something very queer about Miss Porrin these days——
JUDY (*calmly*). She's in love with you.
CORNELIUS (*humorously exaggerating a real note of protest*). Miss Judy Evison! (*He goes towards* JUDY *and stops* C.) You can't

come into this office—this place of business, this commercial establishment—saying things like that.

JUDY. Why not?

CORNELIUS. Because it won't do. It's all wrong. We don't talk like that here. It's not the sort of thing that's going on here.

JUDY. But it's true. I saw it at once. I could have told you on Monday.

CORNELIUS. Well, I'm very glad you didn't tell me on Monday. And I'm sorry you've told me now.

JUDY. So am I, if you feel like that about it. But you wanted to know why she's queer. That's why she's queer. (*She laughs.*) She thinks you're absolutely marvellous.

(CORNELIUS *covers his face with his hand.*)

CORNELIUS (*with rather hastily assumed dignity*). Miss Porrin has been working with me here for some years now——

JUDY (*rising—demurely*). I've finished the letters you gave me, Mr. Cornelius. (*She crosses* C. *to him with wire tray.*) Will you sign them, please?

CORNELIUS. You'd better clear the things off your desk before you go. We shall have to get the place ready for the meeting.

(*He goes into the private office with the letters, leaving the door open slightly.* JUDY *tidies up her desk and begins singing. He returns with the signed letters. She stops singing, but naturally, not suddenly breaking off.*)

Here you are.

(*She goes to him and he hands her the letters.*)

You know, you've got a very pretty voice there, a very pretty voice. Done much singing?

JUDY. I had a few lessons once.

CORNELIUS. You ought to keep on with it.

(JUDY *turns away with the letters, sits at her desk and commences the envelopes.* CORNELIUS *takes out his pipe and looks at it.*)

Wonder if I ought to smoke?

JUDY. Why not?

CORNELIUS. I'm thinking about these creditors. We don't want them coming in here—sniffing—and saying to themselves "Place reeks of tobacco." (*He crosses round up* R.) "These people come here to smoke, not to do business." But then—why should they? I've been a creditor myself in my time, and I never talked like that. (*He laughs.*)

JUDY (*who has just finished her envelopes*). What's the matter?

CORNELIUS (*putting his foot up on the chair* C.). I was just thinking it's a pity we can't give these creditors a good entertainment this afternoon instead of a meeting.

JUDY (*rising—amused*). That would be grand. (*She crosses to* L. *of him.*)

CORNELIUS. You could sing—you sing very nicely, y'know—a very pretty voice there—and I'd—er——

JUDY. Yes, what would you do?

CORNELIUS. I do a very good card trick. The four Jacks represent four commercial travellers. Do you know it? I must show it to you some time. (*He takes his foot off the chair. With a sudden change.*) But you'd better get away to lunch now.

(JUDY *goes to her desk.*)

What do you eat for lunch?

JUDY (*amused*). Oh—all sorts of things. Poached eggs on toast. Or fish-cakes. Or tongue and salad. You know. (*She goes up* L. *to get her hat and coat.*)

CORNELIUS (*looking at her appreciatively*). Yes. Funny. Somehow I can't imagine you eating at all.

JUDY (*laughing*). I eat a lot.

CORNELIUS. Can't imagine it. Now, your sister—though she's not a big girl—I could imagine her tucking into enormous steak-and-kidney puddings and then having two helpings of treacle tart—but you? No. You must let me see you eat some time, will you?

JUDY (*moving down to her desk for bag, gloves and case*). Well, you can if you like, but I don't think you'd find it very amusing. (*She prepares to go.*) Oh—do you want me to come back again—after you've finished the meeting?

CORNELIUS. Well—what do you think?

JUDY (*with obvious reluctance*). I will—if you really want me to. Only——

CORNELIUS. No, no, that's all right. Don't bother.

JUDY (*smiling at him*). Thank you. Good-bye.

(*She goes.* CORNELIUS *crosses slowly to her desk, still smiling at his thought of her. She has left a glove behind on the desk. He picks it up, smooths it out, then contrasts it with his own hand, smiling at the two of them together. While he is doing this,* JUDY *hurries in, rather breathless.*)

(*Coming down to* R. *of him.*) I left a glove. Oh—you've got it.

CORNELIUS (*rather confused*). Yes—I was just wondering whether I could give you a shout down the stairs—and——

JUDY (*smiling*). Here I am. (*Taking the glove.*) Thank you.

(*She hurries out.* CORNELIUS *frowns now, as if dismissing the trivialities of life, and rather importantly surveys the office, obviously trying to decide where to seat the creditors. He crosses* R., *shuts the door and puts the chair* R.C. *to above the swivel chair down* R. *He then goes* C., *takes up a position and begins rehearsing a speech to himself, then changes his position. Then he warms to his work of speechifying, finally saying out loud:* " Gentlemen, I put it to you. You are men of business. So are we." *In the middle of this,* BIDDLE *enters and looks at* CORNELIUS *in mild astonishment.*)

CORNELIUS (*catching sight of him and breaking rather confusedly*). Oh—hello, Biddle. Where's Lawrence?

BIDDLE. Isn't he back yet, sir? He ought to be. (*He begins taking off his coat.*)

CORNELIUS. Of course he ought. Most important afternoon in the whole history of the firm, and we can't get the office boy back in time. Typical typical of the whole—er—of everything nowadays. We must get this place ready for the meeting, Biddle. I was just wondering where to put them.

BIDDLE (*below* MISS PORRIN'S *desk*). I don't suppose they mind where we put 'em, sir, as long as we can promise 'em some money.

CORNELIUS. That's all very well, but there's an art in these things. Put them in one place and they'll all be bad-tempered. Put them in another, and they'll be on our side all the time. Now I think—(*pointing*) over there. Let's see, how many of them will there be?

BIDDLE. Not more than eight, I should say.

CORNELIUS (*looking at the two chairs* R.). Eight would go there nicely. I can see them sitting there, thoroughly pleased with themselves. Now what about chairs?

BIDDLE. This will do for one. (*He takes Judy's chair and puts it in place in front of the other two* R.)

CORNELIUS (*taking* BIDDLE'S *chair to above* JUDY'S). And this for another.

BIDDLE (L.C.). You know, Mr. Cornelius, I don't like that chap the Bank's sending round this afternoon.

CORNELIUS. Who's that? What's-his-name?

BIDDLE. Yes, Mortimer. Don't like him. Very hard, he is.

CORNELIUS. Yes. Got a face like a rat-trap. Probably that's why they send him on these jobs. They know he can make his face like a rat-trap. And yet, you know, Biddle, at home and among his pals, he's probably a very nice fellow. Digs his garden, helps the girls with their homework, plays a good game of bowls, toddles along with his missis to the pictures and pretends to be in love with Greta Garbo—eh? Just an ordinary very nice fellow. Yet he comes along here with a face like a rat-trap. As if owing a bit of money to the Middlesex and Central Bank, when they've got more money than they know what to do with, was a crime so terrible —like murdering children! D'you know what I think sometimes, Biddle?

BIDDLE. No, sir.

CORNELIUS (*very quietly*). Sometimes I think it's all bloody nonsense. (*He sits on the upstage chair* R.C.)

BIDDLE (*crossing* R. *to* CORNELIUS—*rather shocked*). No, Mr. Cornelius. Don't you go thinking that. Whatever you may say, business—well, it's business. You can't change that.

CORNELIUS. I don't know whether I can change it, or whether you can change it, but somebody's always changing it. I've been in business, of one kind and another, for nearly thirty years, and business has never been the same for ten years together. You know that yourself, with your experience.

BIDDLE. Ah—but after all—two and two have still got to make four.

CORNELIUS. They haven't. You ask the Middlesex and Central Bank. Now, two and two have got to make five. And if they had to make four, we couldn't do it, because we haven't got two and two, we've only got two and one. These fellows who are coming here this afternoon, Biddle, they don't want chaps like you as cashiers. They want Einstein.

BIDDLE (*chuckling*). There's something in that.

CORNELIUS. Yes, Einstein as cashier, and Mussolini and Hitler and the storm troops as salesmen.

BIDDLE (*laughing*). Well, I must say I'm very glad to see you in such good spirits, Mr. Cornelius. I've been very worried myself about this afternoon.

CORNELIUS. Have you—so have I.

BIDDLE (*confidentially*). Tell me, sir, what do you think our chances are?

CORNELIUS (*confidentially*). If they'd had to depend on me, Biddle, I'd tell you now our chances were nil. We'd be finished. You know how things stand here.

BIDDLE (*sadly*). Only too well, sir.

CORNELIUS. But they don't depend on me. They depend on Murrison. He's coming back this afternoon, he's going to talk to these fellows, and he's visited every good customer we've ever had. He's not said much in his letters, but I know Bob Murrison, and I know he's coming back with something good up his sleeve.

BIDDLE (*dubiously*). I hope so.

CORNELIUS. When the head of a decent firm like this goes himself—and when he's Bob Murrison, who knows the business inside out, who's got drive, who's got—well—charm, if you like, who they all know to be an absolutely first-class fellow—I tell you—something happens. You'll see.

BIDDLE (*still dubiously*). Yes—I've no doubt you're quite right.

CORNELIUS (*sharply, like a man compelled to face things he wishes to suppress and ignore*). Well, then—what are you talking—looking—like that for? What's the matter with you, Biddle?

BIDDLE (*stammering*). Oh—nothing at all—I'm sure you're quite right, Mr. Cornelius. It was just that Mr. Murrison didn't seem very well when he left us——

CORNELIUS (*rising impatiently*). That's a month ago. He was on edge a bit. (*He crosses* L. *towards the window.*) He was worried. I'm worried. We're all worried. We're all on edge. That's nothing.

BIDDLE. And then—being away so long—and writing so little——

CORNELIUS. You're making something out of nothing. I know him. He wouldn't bother writing much. After all, this is his business, he's no need to explain everything he does to us. He's not like some piffling little salesman out on the road. Besides, Bob Murrison's going to surprise us. I know what he's up to. It won't be the first time. (*At the window.*) I'll bet he's absolutely hypnotized those miserable devils in the North. He's got them eating aluminium out of his hand.

(*Enter* LAWRENCE.)

Where have *you* been all this time?

LAWRENCE (*sulkily*). You told me to go to the Excelsior Transport Company before I came back. (*He hangs up his hat and coat.*)

CORNELIUS (*irritably*). Well, you've been long enough about it. Bring some chairs in from the private office.

(LAWRENCE *goes across to* R. *and stops* R.C.)

And don't look so sulky. I'm tired of seeing you look sulky. Too many miserable, sulky-looking people about.

(LAWRENCE *gives a very audible grunt.*)

Now what does that mean?

(LAWRENCE *stands silent.*)

Well?

LAWRENCE (*flaring up*). It means I'm sick of it.

CORNELIUS (*astonished*). Sick of what?

LAWRENCE. Sick of this place, sick of filling inkwells and copying letters and running silly little errands.

(BIDDLE, *who is upstage* C., *comes down.*)

I've done it nearly five years now. I'm not a kid any longer. I'm nineteen. Lots of my pals have got proper jobs now, and here I am still doing kid's work. Well, I don't care if the firm does go bankrupt. I've had enough of it.

(*He goes into the private office for chairs, leaving* CORNELIUS *to exchange a glance of astonishment with* BIDDLE, *who also shakes his head.* LAWRENCE *returns immediately with two chairs, which he bangs down one at a time on the floor* L. *of* BIDDLE'S *desk.* CORNELIUS, *who is* L. *above* JUDY'S *desk, looks fixedly at him.*)

CORNELIUS (*quietly*). Just a minute, Lawrence.

(LAWRENCE *looks at him and as if almost drawn against his will comes nearer, then stands near.*)

LAWRENCE (*mumbling*). I'm sorry I said that—that last bit, Mr. Cornelius.

CORNELIUS. All right. And I'm sorry we've never had a better job to offer you. If you can find one, go and get it. What do you *want* to do?

LAWRENCE. Something to do with wireless and gramophones. I'm really interested in them.

CORNELIUS. And so is everybody else of your age, as far as I can see. Wireless and gramophones and motor-cars and aeroplanes. Making a noise and rushing off somewhere. And how everybody's going to make a living out of that, beats me. But if you know of anything, go and get it. Go now—if you like.

LAWRENCE. What about the tea?

CORNELIUS. Oh—yes, we shall want that tray of teas.

LAWRENCE. How many?

CORNELIUS. Oh—about eight or nine. Good teas, too. Might make a difference—you never know. About four o'clock. Now you can go, and you needn't come back until you bring the teas.

(LAWRENCE *takes his hat and coat and goes.*)

BIDDLE (*who has been in the background*). Do you want me to stay—or not, Mr. Cornelius? (*He comes down* C. *towards* CORNELIUS.)

CORNELIUS (L.C.). Well, I think you'd better not. You can come back later.

BIDDLE. Of course. I'm anxious to see Mr. Murrison. (*Referring to the chairs.*) Now is this about how you'll want it?

CORNELIUS (*thoughtfully surveying them*). Might just have these two here—(*He moves up and gets the two stools from back, setting them in front of the chairs* LAWRENCE *brought in.*) Like that. (*He goes* R. *and shuts the door.*)

BIDDLE. It's a funny thing, Mr. Cornelius, but to-day's the fifteenth of the month.

CORNELIUS (*still staring at the chairs*). Don't see anything funny about that.

BIDDLE (*laughing*). No, of course. Nothing funny in its being the fifteenth. There has to be a fifteenth. But what's funny is that this is—or may be—an important day in the life of the firm and so an important day in my life. *And* it's the fifteenth. The fifteenth's always been my day. My birthday's on the fifteenth. I was married on the fifteenth. We live at number fifteen.

CORNELIUS (*sitting on the down stage stool*). Oh, you took that house because it was number fifteen. That doesn't count.

BIDDLE. I assure you, we didn't. Just chance, you might say. That is, if there is such a thing as chance, which I doubt. And then, after being a member of our chess club for fifteen years, I took office as President three months ago—on the fifteenth. Now

I've spent a lot of my life dealing with figures and numbers, and I believe there's more in 'em than meets the eye. I do, Mr. Cornelius. Take nine, for instance——

(*There is a sharp knock on the door.* BIDDLE *goes to open it, and admits a youngish foreigner, very sedately dressed, and carrying a black attaché or brief case.* BIDDLE *steps back a pace or two to* R. *of the door and the visitor steps inside the room, bows and produces a card.*)

SCHWEIG (*with very marked foreign accent*). Messrs. Briggs and Murrizon? I am Doc-tor Schweig—coming here for the houz of Hecht and Drapok——

CORNELIUS (*rising, going forward and meeting him* C.). Yes, of course. How d'you do, Doctor—er—Schweig?

(*They shake hands.*)

SCHWEIG. You are Mis-ter Murrizon?
CORNELIUS. No, my name's Cornelius. I'm Mr. Murrison's partner. He'll be back in time for the meeting. We're expecting him any time now. Sit down, won't you?
SCHWEIG (*gravely, crossing in front of* CORNELIUS). T'ank you.

(*He sits down rather ceremoniously on the chair down stage in the front row* R., *keeping his hat and case on his knee.* BIDDLE *is at the window* L. SCHWEIG *takes some files from his case.*)

CORNELIUS. Yes—er—— (*Nothing comes of this.*)
SCHWEIG. It is co-old, eh?
CORNELIUS (C., *eagerly*). Yes, it is cold, isn't it? (*He moves up to* MISS PORRIN'S *desk.*)
BIDDLE (*turning from the window*). Very cold.
CORNELIUS. We were saying that. Very cold.
SCHWEIG. But no fog.
CORNELIUS. No, no fog.
SCHWEIG. Alvays, I am thankful when I am in Lon-don to see no fog.
CORNELIUS. Yes, I can understand that. I say, Biddle, I think we ought to have a table of some sort here. We forgot that. Let's get this desk here.

(*They turn* MISS PORRIN'S *desk from up and down stage to across and put the chair behind it. They have just got this into position when a brisk ratty type of Cockney pops his head in.*)

FLETCHER. This is it, isn't it? Thought so. (*He comes in.*) Mr. Cornelius, isn't it? Central Forwarding Company—Fletcher. (*He crosses* R.) Sit here, I suppose. (*He sits down in the chair behind* SCHWEIG *and turns to him.*) Bit early, are we? Must be.

(BIDDLE *crosses* L. *and puts on his hat and coat.*)

SCHWEIG (*consulting his watch*). I vas told to com' at fifteen minutes past three o'clock. Now it is seventeen minutes past three o'clock.
FLETCHER. Oh, you're making a stop-watch job of it.
SCHWEIG (*puzzled*). Pleass?
FLETCHER. Never mind. Well, Mr. Cornelius, how's everything looking?
CORNELIUS. Fine.
FLETCHER. That's right. Never say die.

(BIDDLE, *who has now put on his hat and coat, reaches the door and opens it to find an elderly man standing outside. This* ELDERLY MAN *has an untidy grey beard and is shabbily dressed in an old-fashioned style. He is carrying a number of leaflets.* BIDDLE *steps back to* R. *to let him in and he comes just inside the door and stands there beaming rather foolishly.*)

ELDERLY MAN (*in the doorway*). Good afternoon, friends.
BIDDLE (R. *of him*). Are you here for the meeting?
ELDERLY MAN. I don't know.
BIDDLE. Do you represent any of the creditors?
ELDERLY MAN. Certainly I do, sir. Certainly I do.
CORNELIUS (*rather irritably*). Well, come and sit down, my dear sir. Don't stand in the doorway.

(*The* ELDERLY MAN *comes to* CORNELIUS C.)

All right, Biddle, don't wait.
ELDERLY MAN (L. *of* CORNELIUS, *very quietly*). I represent the biggest creditor of all, everybody's creditor—God.

(CORNELIUS *stares at him.* FLETCHER *gives a guffaw.*)

FLETCHER. Thought I'd seen him before.

(BIDDLE *goes, after a puzzled backward glance at the* ELDERLY MAN, *who now takes another short step or two forward and continues to beam on the company.*)

He's one o' these sort of apostles you see about, that's what he is.
CORNELIUS. My dear chap, you can't come in here talking to us about God. We're busy. We have an important meeting on. This is business.
ELDERLY MAN. Whose business? Is it God's business? He's here, you know.
FLETCHER. Well, if he's here, we shan't need you. (*He guffaws.*)
ELDERLY MAN (*offering* CORNELIUS *some pamphlets*). Read these at your leisure, friend.
CORNELIUS (*taking them*). All right, thanks, I will. But you'll have to go now——

ELDERLY MAN (*putting a pamphlet on* JUDY'S *desk, and speaking quietly at first*). I am going. I'm young. (*He moves up to* L. *of* MISS PORRIN'S *desk*.) But I wish I could lend you my vision of you, friends, if only for a moment. I see you in a little place—like a very small fragile raft—in mid-air—and heaven is bright above you, bright with your guardian angels—and (*his voice takes on a rather sing-song dramatic tone*) below you—gaping and roaring—is hell and eternal damnation.

FLETCHER. Oh—gertcha!

CORNELIUS (*as if about to push him out*). My dear chap, we simply can't have you here talking——

ELDERLY MAN (*who has reached the door and opened it*). Friends,—

(CORNELIUS *turns away*.)

—I leave with you the thought of our Father in Heaven.

(MRS. READE, *a fussily dressed woman of about forty, is seen behind him. He too sees her*.)

(*Forcing a pamphlet on her.*) And with you too, sister. (*He goes to* L. *of her*.)

MRS. READE. Me what?

ELDERLY MAN. The thought of our Father in Heaven.

(*He brushes past her. She looks after him for a second, flustered and indignant, then comes a step or so into the room*.)

MRS. READE. Oh—he gave me quite a turn with his Father in Heaven. They oughtn't to let old men go about talking like that. (*She puts the pamphlet on* JUDY'S *desk*.)

SCHWEIG (*rising, gravely*). Quite so, madame. In my country he would be shut up as a madman.

CORNELIUS. Oh—no. You can't do that.

SCHWEIG. But he is mad.

CORNELIUS. A bit mad. But most of us are a bit mad here. Where you come from, it's probably different.

MRS. READE (*with social manner*). I ought to have introduced myself. This is where you're having the creditors' meeting, isn't it?

CORNELIUS (*staring at her*). Yes. But——

MRS. READE. Well, I'm Mrs. Reade. Oh! I don't suppose that means much to you, does it? But my uncle, Mr. Samuel Rigby—I keep house for him—he owns this property.

(CORNELIUS *starts to back* R., *with* MRS. READE *following*.)

You're his tenants, you see. And he couldn't come himself—he's got a bit of sciatica to-day—he told me about this meeting this morning. And so I said: "Well, Uncle, let me go. I've never been to such a thing before and I can tell you what happens and it'll be a bit of a change." (*She is* R.) And he said I could if I wanted to. So I did. I can sit anywhere, I suppose?

CORNELIUS (*rather wearily*). Yes, anywhere.

MRS. READE (*sitting in the chair above* SCHWEIG). I think I'll try this.

(*She looks about her, and smiles at* SCHWEIG *and* FLETCHER. COR-NELIUS *looks impatiently at his watch, then goes into the private office, leaving the door ajar behind him.*)

(*After clearing her throat.*) Well, we're having a nice day for it, aren't we? I mean, taking it all round. It's cold—but it's what I should call a healthy cold.

FLETCHER (*indifferently*). It's what I should call it too. (*He pulls a bit of paper out of his inner pocket and begins examining some figures written on it.*)

MRS. READE (*mainly to* SCHWEIG). I expect you gentlemen are used to this sort of thing, but it's quite new to me. A brand-new experience, you might call it.

SCHWEIG (*not taking it in*). Pleass?

MRS. READE (*brightly*). Yes, you're foreign, aren't you? I guessed you were.

(*The telephone bell rings.*)

There, that's the telephone. Always at it. Ring, ring, ring.

(CORNELIUS *comes out hastily from the private office. He shuts the door and goes to the telephone.*)

CORNELIUS (*eagerly, at telephone*). That you, Bob? (*Disappointed.*) Oh! No, we're not interested. Not interested. (*He puts the receiver down.*)

(*Here, if it is convenient to have one or two nondescript creditors—youngish or middle-aged men—they should enter, and quietly take their seats. They are followed by* PRITCHET *and* MORTIMER. PRITCHET *is a middle-aged solicitor, with one of those curiously hollow booming voices that some legal men have.* MORTIMER *is the bank man with the face like a rat-trap. He should have a worrying, ratty manner. Both carry small cases.*)

PRITCHET (*booming*). Ah good afternoon. Sorry if we're a little late. I'm Pritchet of Cattermole, MacIvor and Pritchet. (*Going nearer to* CORNELIUS *and producing a slip of paper.*) We represent several foreign clients who are er—interested in these proceedings. You'll find their names there—eh?

CORNELIUS (*glancing at the paper*). Yes. Old friends of ours. Good afternoon, Mr. Mortimer.

MORTIMER. Good afternoon, Mr. Cornelius.

CORNELIUS. Sit down, gentlemen.

The positions are:—

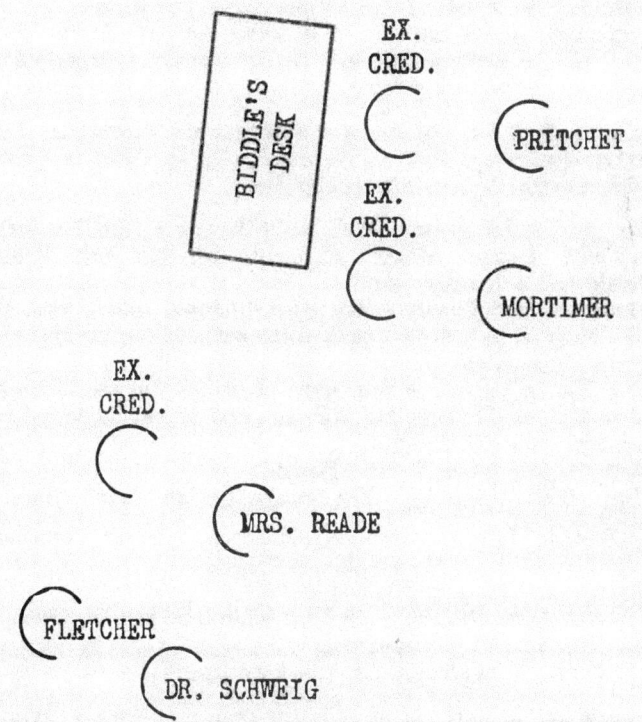

(*As they sit,* Mrs. Reade's *voice can be heard.*)

Mrs. Reade. Do you think we're all here now?

Cornelius. That's what I was wondering, madam. I think I can take it that we are. (*He goes to door, looks out, then closes the door and carefully and rather importantly takes up a position above* Miss Porrin's *desk and facing the creditors.*) Gentlemen—I beg your pardon, madam——

Mrs. Reade (*flattered by this notice*). It's quite all right, thank you.

Cornelius (*grandly*). Gentlemen and you, madam—I propose first to outline our position to you. Three years ago——

Pritchet (*rising and booming unpleasantly*). One moment, please.

Cornelius. What's the matter?

Pritchet. This is not quite in order.

Cornelius (*taken aback*). Oh!

Pritchet. No. This is a meeting of your creditors, my dear sir. You are not one of your own creditors. Therefore you can't take charge of the meeting in this manner.

Fletcher. That's right.

PRITCHET. I propose that Mr. Mortimer of the Middlesex and Central Bank should take the chair.
FLETCHER (*bobbing up and down*). And I beg to second that.
PRITCHET. All in agreement?

(*A few hands go up.*)

Carried, I think.

(MRS. READE *puts her hand up.*)

Mr. Mortimer, will you please take charge of the meeting? (*He sits again.*)

(MORTIMER, *silent, goes forward in front of* CORNELIUS *and occupies the chair at* MISS PORRIN'S *desk, putting it away a little first, so that* CORNELIUS *is left, so to speak, in the air.*)

CORNELIUS (*not without irony*). What do I do now? Leave the room? (*He stands* R. *of the desk.*)
MRS. READE (*whispering loudly*). I hope not. I like him.
MORTIMER. I don't think that will be necessary just now. Do you, Mr. Pritchet?
PRITCHET. No, not yet.
MORTIMER. Is your partner, Mr. Murrison, here, Mr. Cornelius?
CORNELIUS. No.
MORTIMER. But I understood——
CORNELIUS (*impatiently*). Mr. Murrison will be here any moment now. (*He crosses* L. *to the window.*)
PRITCHET. This seems to me all very irregular——
CORNELIUS (*bitterly*). That's how it seems to me too, very irregular. Everything's irregular. That's why we're all here to-day.
FLETCHER. Only we're not all here. Your partner isn't, for one—— (*He sniffs.*)
CORNELIUS. My partner has been travelling the country for the last few weeks. He's been visiting all our customers, chiefly in the Midlands and the North. He's coming straight back from seeing the last of them to this meeting this afternoon.
SCHWEIG. He hopes to get more orders for your houz, eh?
CORNELIUS. Yes. He knows all there is to know about the aluminium trade.
MRS. READE. The what?
CORNELIUS. The aluminium trade, madam. This firm imports aluminium from abroad and sells it to hardware manufacturers.
MRS. READE. Just fancy!
MORTIMER. But don't you employ a traveller?
PRITCHET. Just what I was about to ask, Mr. Mortimer.
CORNELIUS. We had a traveller, but about two months ago we dismissed him.
FLETCHER. What for?
MORTIMER. Was he inefficient?

CORNELIUS. He wasn't at first——
PRITCHET. But he was afterwards, eh?
CORNELIUS. I don't know.
PRITCHET (*rising*). But, my dear sir, surely it's not difficult to discover whether an employee of this kind is efficient or not? (*He sits again.*)
FLETCHER. 'Ear, 'ear!
CORNELIUS. At ordinary times I suppose it isn't, but in our business these aren't ordinary times. This fellow was a traveller, not a magician.
FLETCHER. And what about your partner, Murrison, then? Is he a magician?
CORNELIUS. *Mister* Murrison is a first-class business man and a wonderful fellow. And this little firm means everything to him. If it hadn't, he wouldn't have gone on this trip. He wasn't very well when he went. We'd had an anxious time here——
MORTIMER (*impatiently*). Yes, yes, Mr. Cornelius, we've all had anxious times. But meanwhile, we're busy men.
PRITCHET. Quite so.
CORNELIUS. Just a minute! (*He listens.*) All right. Sorry!
PRITCHET. I must say if I'd known that your senior partner was absent——
CORNELIUS. He knows about this. He'll be here any minute now.
FLETCHER (*sceptically*). With luck.
CORNELIUS (*crossing to* C.). What do you mean?
FLETCHER. You 'eard me.
CORNELIUS. I resent that remark, particularly from you.
FLETCHER (*pugnaciously*). Oh—(*half-rising*) and why from me?
CORNELIUS. Because . . . you wouldn't understand if I told you. (*He crosses to the door* L. *and looks off.*)
MORTIMER (*rapping on the desk*). Gentlemen, this is a business meeting. We don't want that sort of talk.
PRITCHET. I should think not indeed. How long is this Mr. Murrison going to be?
FLETCHER. God knows.
MORTIMER. I'm not prepared to wait more than ten minutes at the outside——
PRITCHET. Nor I.
CORNELIUS (*returning to* L.C.). I tell you he'll be here any minute now.
SCHWEIG (*standing up*). Mister—er—Cornelius wass going to gif us a stademendt—some figures—of the position of the houz. I think he might gif us that stademendt—pleass. (*He sits down.*)
CORNELIUS (*eagerly*). Yes, of course.
MORTIMER. All right, Mr. Cornelius.

(CORNELIUS *produces the paper given to him by* MISS PORRIN *and moves to* R. *of* MISS PORRIN'S *desk.*)

CORNELIUS. Well, gentlemen—and you, madam—up to three years ago, our annual gross turnover, averaged over the previous five years, was eighty-five thousand pounds——

SCHWEIG (*who is writing it down*). Pleass ? Eighty-five t'ousand pounds ?

CORNELIUS. Eighty-five thousand pounds, with an annual net profit ranging from eleven thousand pounds at the beginning of the period to about eight thousand at the end—— (*He pauses.*)

SCHWEIG (*murmuring as he writes*). Eleven t'ousand pounds to eight t'ousand pounds.

CORNELIUS (*reminiscently*). We were doing very well. We were very fine people. It was a good life. You were always delighted to see us at the Middlesex and Central Bank, Mr. Mortimer. Those French clients of yours, Mr. Pritchet, used to send us little presents. Mr. Fletcher here and his Forwarding Company couldn't do enough for us. You all respected us. And really, gentlemen, now I come to think of it, I don't know why you should all have been so affable and respectful then. It was all very easy. We bought the metal, turned it over to our customers, made a nice profit. All very easy, very simple, nothing to boast about at all. (*He looks round, smiling, and catches* MRS. READE'S *eye.*)

MRS. READE (*brightly*). No, I see.

CORNELIUS (*impressively*). Thank you, madam. And then it all changed. My God—how it changed ! A sort of nightmare. Every country seemed to be announcing that it must sell more goods than it would buy.

MORTIMER. Isn't this all rather beside the point ?

PRITCHET. Hear, hear !

CORNELIUS (*with increasing animation*). It may be beside the point in the Middlesex and Central Bank or near the Law Courts, but it isn't beside the point here. Look what happened. The pound sterling was worth twenty shillings here and only twelve shillings somewhere else. Some countries you couldn't get money into. Some countries you couldn't get money out of. You could send goods in a ship with a blue flag but not in a ship with a red flag. It wasn't business any more. It was a game of snakes and ladders—but without the ladders.

PRITCHET. I really don't see——

CORNELIUS. All right, don't see. But you've got to understand what was happening to us. I've never got much fun out of selling aluminium. And whether Briggs and Murrison of Birdcage Street, Holborn, ever sold any aluminium to anybody couldn't be of any real importance to the world. But—by God !—if we'd been trying to take a lifeboat out to a wreck, we couldn't have tried harder, couldn't have worried and argued and schemed and pleaded more than we did in this office. And what's it all about ? If we've to live by private trade, then let it be private trade. Why have they made it like a lunatics' obstacle race ? Why are we condemned to scheme and scratch in these cubby holes? I tell you, a blind monkey could find a better life to live than we've lately had here .

MORTIMER (*sharply*). Mr. Cornelius.

PRITCHET (*sharply*). I thought you were going to give us a statement.

CORNELIUS. I am. (*Deliberately.*) Unless my partner's been working miracles—and I don't say he hasn't, because he's a desperate man and a wonder—but unless he's worked a few miracles, this firm's broke, bankrupt, bust. And now you can pass a few resolutions on that.

(*He holds it a moment, during which his audience, aghast, can only gape at him. Then he turns away to the door and goes out, holding it open.* MRS. READE *breaks the spell.*)

MRS. READE. Well, I enjoyed that, I must say.

FLETCHER. I can't see what that stuff's got to do with us——

PRITCHET. I really must protest very strongly against this most unbusinesslike proceeding——

MORTIMER. Mr. Cornelius, you haven't made any attempt to give us a statement——

CORNELIUS (*holding up his hand, forcefully*). Just a minute, just a minute——

(*He listens in the quiet that follows. The creditors watch him and a low buzz of talk breaks out amongst them.* CORNELIUS *sees* MURRISON. MURRISON *is a man about fifty, who is looking very worn. He is wearing a big overcoat and carrying his hat in his hand. His manner from the first should be quick, nervous, jerky, strange.*)

(*Outside, with affectionate warmth.*) Hello, Bob, old boy! Fine! (*Following* MURRISON *in.*) We're all ready for you.

MURRISON (*now inside the room, with a quick glance at the creditors, sharply*). What? What d'you mean?

CORNELIUS. The meeting, y'know. Did you come straight from the station, Bob? (*He stands* R. *of* MURRISON.)

MURRISON. Yes. Straight from the station. The taximan's bringing my bags up. (*Whispering.*) You see him out there, Jim, and pay him for me. I don't like the look of him.

CORNELIUS (*hastily concealing his surprise and some misgivings*). Of course I will, old boy.

(CORNELIUS *goes out, and is heard off calling to the taximan:* "Put them down just in here, will you? That's right. How much? Here you are." *Meanwhile,* MURRISON *has very carefully crossed to the private office door, ignoring the* "Good afternoon, Mr. Murrison" *of* MR. MORTIMER. MURRISON *goes into the private office, so that for a moment or two the creditors are left to themselves.* MORTIMER *is seen exchanging a puzzled glance with* PRITCHET. CORNELIUS *returns, looks for* MURRISON, *then goes over to the private office. The creditors have all looked round as* MURRISON *crosses and goes off* R. *and do so again when* CORNELIUS *does the same. There should be an atmosphere of suspense and tension evoked in this little scene.*)

(*Looking into the private office.*) Ready, Bob?

(*He goes to the alcove at the back and brings down the only remaining chair, putting it behind the desk and* R. *of* MORTIMER. MURRISON *slowly opens the door and enters hesitatingly. He has taken his overcoat off.*)

Here you are. Sit here, Bob.

MURRISON (*in a loud harsh voice that is startling*). Why are you sitting like this? We want the lights on. Pull that blind down, Jim. I'll put the lights on.

(CORNELIUS, *after a brief surprised look at* MURRISON, *hastily goes to the window and pulls down the blind.* MURRISON *goes to the switch* L. *and puts on the lights.*)

(*Irritably.*) There's another light somewhere.

MORTIMER. Come, come, Mr. Murrison, we've got plenty of light in here now.

MURRISON (*irritably*). I want that other light on. (*He crosses* R. *and turns on the other light over the door* R.)

(*There is now the maximum of light on the stage and it is almost an uncomfortable glare, the lights being very white. Coming back from switching on the last light,* MURRISON *stops and looks searchingly at* MRS. READE.)

What's that woman doing here? (*He crosses to* CORNELIUS, *who is* L.)

CORNELIUS. That's all right, old man. She's only the landlord's niece——

MRS. READE (*who is suddenly alarmed and has risen*). You needn't bother telling him who I am. Because I'm going. (*As she threads her way towards the door* L., *agitatedly.*) And you might as well all go, if you'll take my advice. It's no good staying here —with that man. (*She indicates* MURRISON.)

(*She is now at the door. Her voice rises and trembles as she points at* MURRISON, *who is still looking at her.*)

You've only got to look at him to see—— (*She half-chokes, and gasps.*)

(*She goes hastily, the door banging to. Some of the creditors, who have half-risen, remain like that for a moment.*)

CORNELIUS (*reassuringly, as he crosses to* C.). That's all right. She's better out of the way. We can get on now.

MORTIMER (*who has been bewildered*). I hope so. (*Looking at his watch.*) Really, gentlemen, I must ask you——

CORNELIUS (*cutting in, to* MURRISON). Bob, you'd better tell them at once what you've been able to do.

(MURRISON *sits in the chair* CORNELIUS *has brought down for him.* CORNELIUS *goes and stands* R. *of him.*)

MURRISON (*in a low uncertain tone*). It's very difficult. (*He covers his face with his hands for a moment.*) There were two men following me all the time. No, not all the time. Not at first. But nearly all the time.

CORNELIUS (*bewildered*). Following you!

MURRISON (*rather louder now*). Everywhere I went. When I went up to Scotland, one of them tried to get into my railway carriage. But I knew him. (*He looks round suspiciously.*) How did they always know where I was going?

MORTIMER (*firmly*). Well, never mind about that for the time being, Mr. Murrison. We understand that you've been visiting all your customers. And naturally before we reach any conclusion here, we want to hear the result of those visits.

CORNELIUS. Yes. How did you get on, old man? Tell us.

MURRISON (*with passion*). I am telling you. I'm telling you that everywhere I went, I was followed by two men.

(*There is an exchange of looks between the creditors.*)

And there were—other things. (*His voice dropping.*) Worse than that. They tried to poison my food.

CORNELIUS (*expostulating*). Bob!

MURRISON (*excitedly*). They knew where I was going all the time. They sent somebody in advance to all the people who'd been buying from us. Some of our oldest customers wouldn't see me. Why? Because they'd been told filthy lies about us by this fellow who'd been sent ahead of me. I tell you—it's been hell.

FLETCHER (*disgustedly*). Here, come off it!

SCHWEIG (*standing up*). I think, pleass——

MURRISON (*quickly*). Who's that?

(SCHWEIG *sits down.*)

Some sort of foreigner, isn't he? Why should he come here?

CORNELIUS (*patting him on the shoulder*). Bob, old man, you're tired. Take it easy.

MURRISON. You'd be tired. Followed, watched, spied on, day after day. Trying to get at you. There was something about it in the paper yesterday. I expect you'll be reading a lot about it in the papers soon. They'll try to get at me here. They won't leave me alone—— (*Beginning to break down.*) Oh God!—why can't they leave me alone?

CORNELIUS (*bending over him*). It's all right, old man, now. You've nothing to worry about.

(*There is a pause.* CORNELIUS *looks up, and makes a waving gesture to the creditors for them to go, then looks down again.*)

You're only a bit done up. You'll be all right after a rest.

(FLETCHER *and another creditor have risen.*)

(*To the creditors, in a low rather tense tone.*) I'm sorry, gentlemen, but I must ask you to go.

(*Some of the other creditors get up, but nobody makes for the door. They are all staring at* MURRISON, *who is sitting with his head between his hands.*)

MURRISON (*not raising his head*). It's no use, Jim. I'm finished. They're torturing me. (*He breaks down again.*)

CORNELIUS (*very gently, bending over him*). No, no, no. That's all right, Bob old man. (*He looks up and sees the creditors watching them. Then, with tremendous passion.*) For Christ's sake—get out, can't you?

(*As if completely dominated by his will and passion, they begin to move towards the door at once. As soon as he sees that they are all on the move, he turns away from them and bends over* MURRISON, *who is still sitting with bowed head. Nothing is said until they are alone.*)

MURRISON (*raising his head and suddenly giving a short harsh laugh*). They've all gone, you see. (*He laughs again.*) I got rid of them, Jim. It wasn't hard. But it took me to do it, eh? (*He laughs.*)

CORNELIUS (*standing at the back and staring*). What, are you all right, Bob?

MURRISON (*irritably; rising*). Of course I am. Why shouldn't I be?

CORNELIUS (*relieved, breaking round up* R.). My dear chap, I don't know what the devil you were playing at with those fellows. (*Crossing to him.*) And I don't care so long as you're all right. (*He claps him heartily on the shoulder.*)

MURRISON (*sharply*). Don't do that.

CORNELIUS. Sorry, old man. I expect you're tired.

MURRISON (*slowly; sitting again*). No, but—nearly all the time—I have a pain here. (*He puts his hand to the top of his head.*)

CORNELIUS (*heartily*). Really? How did you get that?

MURRISON (*solemnly and emphatically*). Some sort of poison, Jim. Didn't I tell you?

CORNELIUS. No. But tell me now how you got on? Have we got a chance?

MURRISON (*shaking his head, irritably*). I've already told you. They sent somebody in advance—to warn all the customers——

CORNELIUS. But who did?

MURRISON. I told you. I was followed all the time. There were two men——

CORNELIUS (*taking him by the shoulders, earnestly*). Now! Now! For God's sake, Bob, stop talking like that. You're talking to me now, Jim Cornelius. There couldn't have been two men following you all the time. You imagined it.

MURRISON (*withdrawing himself, sharply*). That's a lie. You know it's a lie.

CORNELIUS (*on whom the horrible truth is dawning again*). No, I don't.

MURRISON. Are you going to begin lying to me now, Jim? Won't anybody tell me the truth? (*Confusedly.*) There was a waiter in the hotel last night—he looked a decent sort of chap—but when I asked him if anybody had been trying to tamper with my drink—he wouldn't tell me the truth. And I knew all the time. He ought to have seen that. (*He laughs.*) I knew.

CORNELIUS (*agonized, under his breath*). Oh—God! (*He turns away, then approaching* MURRISON *again.*) Don't talk like that, old man. Please. Just for my sake.

(LAWRENCE *enters* L., *rather proudly, carrying a large tray, on which are about nine cups of tea and a plate of cut cake and biscuits. He is out of breath.*)

MURRISON (*suspiciously, sharply*). What's this? I don't want any tea.

CORNELIUS (*impatiently*). Take it away.

LAWRENCE (*gasping*). But—where—to?

CORNELIUS. Anywhere—anywhere—back to the teashop.

LAWRENCE. They'll—want—paying for it.

CORNELIUS. Oh—all right—take this——

(*He goes over and throws half a crown on to the tray. After a curious stare at* MURRISON, LAWRENCE *goes out.* CORNELIUS *returns to* R. *of* MURRISON.)

Bob, will you listen to me—quietly—for a minute?

MURRISON (*sullenly*). What is it?

CORNELIUS. It doesn't matter just now what's going to happen to us here. Never mind about that. You're tired. You're not well. This journey's upset you. Go home now—never mind about business—and just see your doctor, old man. Tell him about this pain in your head.

MURRISON (*rising and slowly shaking his head*). No. No. He wouldn't believe me.

CORNELIUS. Why not?

MURRISON (*with a sinister air of secrecy*). I've never liked that doctor of ours, Jim. Once or twice, when he thought I wasn't noticing, I've caught him looking very strangely at me. I couldn't trust him.

CORNELIUS (*now deeply distressed*). But you can trust me, can't you, Bob? We've been partners, we've been pals, for a good long time now. You know there isn't anything I wouldn't do for you, old man. And I don't like to see you ill—like this. We need you down here, Bob. We can't get on without you. So if you really don't like this doctor of yours, see another one—there are plenty about, good ones, too——

MURRISON. It's no use, Jim. It's no use.

CORNELIUS (*with deep affection*). Of course it is. Think of the good times we've had together—even here, in this office. And we'll have some more, won't we? If we can't keep this business going, we'll get out of it somehow and start another—something quite different. What do you say?

(*There is a noise outside.*)

MURRISON (*startled*). What's that?

(BIDDLE *enters.*)

BIDDLE. Hello, Mr. Murrison. I nearly fell over your bags out there.

(CORNELIUS, *behind* MURRISON, *puts his hand to his mouth as a sign to* BIDDLE *to keep quiet.*)

CORNELIUS. You'll do that, won't you, Bob?

MURRISON. All right. (*He fumbles in his pockets, finally producing some keys.*) There's something I want, first.

(*He goes into the private office.* CORNELIUS *immediately crosses to* BIDDLE.)

BIDDLE (*anxiously*). Is anything wrong, sir?

CORNELIUS (*quickly and softly*). Yes, but there's no time to explain. (*Hurrying* BIDDLE *towards the door* L.) Go out and get a taxi for Mr. Murrison, and then telephone at once—from that box at the corner—to his house, tell them he's coming home and ask them to get a good doctor in to see him, as he's not very well. That clear?

BIDDLE (*softly*). Yes. Taxi, then telephone.

(MURRISON *has come out of the private office, carrying a rather bright revolver in his hand. He holds it just long enough to be seen, then slips it into his pocket.*)

And he'll want the bags in, of course.

MURRISON (*as* BIDDLE *moves off*). What are you two muttering about there?

CORNELIUS (*with forced cheerfulness*). Nothing, old man. I was just asking Biddle to get you a taxi.

MURRISON (*sitting down heavily on the chair occupied by* MRS. READE *at the meeting—wearily*). No use, Jim, no use. (*He puts his hand to his head, then shakes it.*) Talk to me—about something different. Tell me something about yourself, Jim. Anything. Just talk.

CORNELIUS (*trying to hide his distress*). All right, Bob. (*He brings down the chair from above* MISS PORRIN'S *desk to* L. *of* MURRISON.) You know, I'm reading a book about South America—Peru and the Andes. It's making me feel restless, making me wonder a lot, about what I've missed. You know the feeling, old man. Right on the first page, there was a sentence . . . I keep remembering it, Bob—you know how you remember some things for no reason at all. . . . It said——

(*Now* MURRISON *is leaning forward, staring tragically into vacancy while* CORNELIUS *has an affectionate hand on his shoulder.*)

"After a week in the Indian village, we decided to take the track into the clouds, to find among those heights the lost city of the Incas . . ."

CURTAIN.

ACT III

The Office. Friday evening, a fortnight later.
(For slight alteration in the setting see Property Plot.)
The office is partly dismantled. Files and ledgers taken down from shelves, stacked in corners, some tied in bundles. The staff are obviously at work clearing things up for the last time. The door into the private office is open and a light is on in there. LAWRENCE *is bringing files, etc., from the private office.* MISS PORRIN *can be looking through files.* BIDDLE *is having a last go at the ledgers.* JUDY *is at her table typing hard. Nothing is said for a few moments.*

LAWRENCE (*stopping and yawning*). What time is it?

(*There is no reply.*)

Miss Porrin, what time is it? (*He puts a file into the* L. *basket.*)
MISS PORRIN. Twenty to eight.

(LAWRENCE *whistles.*)

LAWRENCE. I've had enough of this. (*He puts another file into the basket.*)

MISS PORRIN (*indignantly*). You ought to be ashamed of yourself, Lawrence.

LAWRENCE (*astonished*). What for? (*He puts the third file into the basket.*)

MISS PORRIN. On an evening like this—when everything's finishing—and you talk as if it didn't matter a bit——

LAWRENCE (*taking a ledger from table* C. *to* MISS PORRIN). Well, it doesn't to me.

MISS PORRIN (*putting a letter from the file into her basket*). I think you're absolutely inhuman.

LAWRENCE (*muttering*). And I think you're potty. (*He goes up and brings a book from the desk to the table* C., *then backwards and forwards again.*)

MISS PORRIN. Don't be so rude and stupid. You ought to realize that even if you don't care about—about—all this (*rising and moving down to* LAWRENCE *at the table*), the rest of us do because it means a lot to us and——

BIDDLE (*turning*). What's all this about? (*He rises and dumps a ledger on the piles at the table* C.)

(LAWRENCE *returns to the desk at back.*)

MISS PORRIN. I'm sorry, Mr. Biddle. But it's Lawrence—

being so rude and stupid. He ought to know I can't help feeling upset, because this is really our last night here——

(BIDDLE *has returned to his desk*.)

VOICE OF CORNELIUS (*from the private office, quietly*). Not so much noise in there, please.

(LAWRENCE *grins at* MISS PORRIN, *who returns to her work*.)

Lawrence!

(LAWRENCE *goes in and returns with a parcel of papers which he dumps on the floor below* MISS PORRIN'S *desk. Then he yawns noisily*.)

JUDY (*with calm malice*). Is it the little boy's bedtime?
LAWRENCE. Don't be silly. I'm yawning because I need fresh air. I can't help it. (*He goes up to the back for more books*.)
JUDY. Put your head out of the window.
MISS PORRIN. Oh—do please, stop it!
LAWRENCE. Well, I didn't start it, did I?

(*He puts the books on* MISS PORRIN'S *desk and goes to the back again. The telephone rings*. MISS PORRIN *answers it*.)

MISS PORRIN. Yes, Briggs and Murrison. . . . All right. Wait a minute, please. Miss Evison, it's for you.

(LAWRENCE *grins as* JUDY *crosses to the 'phone*.)

JUDY (*at telephone*). Yes, this is Judy . . . I know, Eric, I'm awfully sorry, but I can't help it . . . No, I shan't be long. If you come round here, you probably won't have to wait more than a few minutes.

(MISS PORRIN *comes down and drops books on piles*.)

. . . Of course I will, darling. (*She puts down the receiver and starts to return to her desk*.)

LAWRENCE (*getting up from putting books on the floor and muttering contemptuously*). Darling!
JUDY (*going up to him*). What did you say?
LAWRENCE (*quailing*). Nothing. (*He goes up to the desk at back*.)

(JUDY *returns to her desk*.)

BIDDLE (*looking up thoughtfully from his account books*). Some very queer things in these old accounts. In December nineteen twenty-two we spent fifteen shillings and threepence on cheese.
JUDY. Cheese? (*She laughs*.)
BIDDLE. Yes, cheese. (*To* MISS PORRIN.) How did we come to do that? Why should we buy cheese? And fifteen shillings and threepence worth. You could get a lot of cheese for that. Do you remember, Miss Porrin?
MISS PORRIN. No, I wasn't here then.

BIDDLE (*thoughtfully*). Of course not. I must ask my wife. I expect I told her at the time. It'll worry me if I can't remember. Cheese. Nineteen twenty-two. Lot of queer things here.

MISS PORRIN. Here too. (*Rising and moving across to* BIDDLE *with a file.*) I never knew before that Mr. Shuttleworth—you know, of the Central Forwarding Company—was called Michael. He's not a bit like a Michael, is he?

BIDDLE. Isn't he? I don't know what a Michael should be like.

JUDY (*without looking up*). Tall, dark, and very romantic.

BIDDLE. That doesn't sound like Mr. Shuttleworth.

(MISS PORRIN *empties the file into a basket and returns to* L. *of her desk. A pause. Then* CORNELIUS *appears in the doorway of the private office, with a cigar-box in his hand. He is wearing a dark suit and a black tie, and shows signs of having had a bad time. He moves to below* BIDDLE'S *desk and speaks very quietly.*)

CORNELIUS. Look at these, Biddle.

(BIDDLE *rises and moves round to* L. *of him.*)

Nearly a full box of those big Zarranagas. Must have been at the bottom of that drawer years and years. Isn't it a shame?

(MISS PORRIN *goes up to desk at back.*)

BIDDLE (*taking out big but ragged cigar gravely*). It is a shame, Mr. Cornelius. These must have been expensive cigars.

CORNELIUS. Cost about half a crown each.

BIDDLE (*impressed*). Half a crown! (*Peering into the box.*)

CORNELIUS. Take them, Biddle, if you think you can do anything with 'em. They look hopeless to me.

BIDDLE (*taking them*). Oh—thank you. I think if they're trimmed up a bit, they'll make a very good smoke, a very good smoke.

CORNELIUS. Then your commercial career, Biddle, ends in smoke, but in very good smoke.

(BIDDLE *returns to his desk.*)

Lawrence, you'd better clear up some of that mess in there. Then you can go. Look, start on the table first.

(*They go in to the private office together.*)

BIDDLE (*quietly as he returns to his desk with cigars*). Mr. Murrison bought these. He liked a good cigar.

(*There is a tiny knock on the door, then it opens to admit the head and shoulders of* MRS. READE.)

MRS. READE. Oh—good evening. May I come in a minute?

(*She enters, but not far.*)

BIDDLE. Oh—good evening.

Mrs. Reade (*just inside the door*). I'm Mrs. Reade, y'know. The landlord, Mr. Samuel Rigby's my uncle. I've just been up to the top floor—there's a proper private flat there, y'know, we let it out—and I saw a light here and I thought I'd just—(*staring about her*)—you look as if you're going for good.

Biddle. We are. The landlord knows.

Mrs. Reade. Yes, I expect so, but he never tells me anything, even if I do keep house for him. (*She moves to above* L. *of table.*) But what I really called for—is the tall gentleman here I saw the other day at that meeting? Oh, I think he's in there, isn't he? (*Calling.*) Good evening.

Cornelius (*coming out of private office with some things belonging to* Murrison—*flask, personal diary and revolver*). Good evening. (*Puzzled a moment.*) Oh—yes—you're——

Mrs. Reade. Mrs. Reade, that's right. (*Moving* C. *to* Cornelius.) I was at the meeting here, you remember. We've been away since—my uncle had a bit of sciatica—and I've been wondering what happened after that meeting. You know, I couldn't have stayed another minute, not if you'd paid me a thousand pounds. I left, all of a sudden. You remember?

Cornelius (*tonelessly*). Yes, I remember.

(Judy *looks up.*)

Mrs. Reade. That friend of yours—he frightened me.

(Biddle *and* Miss Porrin *stop work and look up at* Mrs. Reade.)

Cornelius. I'm sorry.

Mrs. Reade (*confidentially*). Wasn't he—a bit mad?

Cornelius. Yes.

Mrs. Reade. I knew it. Did they put him away?

Cornelius. No.

Mrs. Reade. Oh—what happened then?

Cornelius (*very gently*). He shot himself.

Mrs. Reade. Shot himself?

Cornelius. Yes. (*Showing the revolver.*) With this.

Mrs. Reade (*recoiling slightly*). Oh, how awful! You must have been very upset.

Cornelius. He was my partner and my best friend.

Mrs. Reade (*curious and consolatory*). I don't suppose he knew what he was doing——

Cornelius. I think he did.

Mrs. Reade. When did this happen?

Cornelius. Ten days ago.

Mrs. Reade. Not—here?

Cornelius. No.

Mrs. Reade. Was he——?

Judy (*jumping up with startling effect*). Oh—do stop! How can you stand there asking these idiotic questions?

Mrs. Reade (*indignantly*). What do you mean? (*She takes a step towards* Judy.)

Judy. I mean that there's been quite enough of it already. Can't you see you're hurting him—and making us all want to scream?

Cornelius (*gently*). Judy!

Judy. I'm sorry—but you ought to have seen it for yourself. (*She sits and begins putting her typed sheets together, trying to calm herself.*)

Cornelius (*to* Mrs. Reade, *courteously*). Good night, madam.

Mrs. Reade (*after a final glare at* Judy). Oh—good night.

(*She goes out, leaving the others rigid and silent. Then* Cornelius *puts down on the table the things he has been carrying, and puts away the revolver in a drawer, which must be prominently placed. The silence can be broken here by a dull sort of suppressed sob from* Miss Porrin.)

Cornelius (*above the door* R. *again, looking into the private office*). I don't know you can really do much good there, Lawrence. It's beginning to look like a dustman's job. You'd better clear off, I think. Biddle, you don't want Lawrence for anything, do you?

Biddle. Aren't there some letters going out, Mr. Cornelius? He'd better copy them.

Cornelius (*moving up to* L. *of* Biddle's *desk and speaking with some irony*). There are some letters going out, but I don't think we need copy them.

Biddle (*surprised*). No copies?

Cornelius. No copies. For once, we'll risk it. We don't know what we've said. Just gone—like that. It doesn't matter. They're good letters, but they're not meant to be answered. Perhaps the best letters are never meant to be answered. They're certainly never meant to be copied.

(Lawrence *comes out.*)

(*Moving down* L.C.) Well, Lawrence, at last you'll be able to make a fresh start in life, eh?

Lawrence (*shyly*). Yes, sir.

Cornelius (*seriously*). I'm sorry we've wasted your time. But you know we've wasted a lot of our own time too. And we haven't as much to spare as you have. What's it to be? (*He moves down stage and across to* R.)

Lawrence (*with a rush of confidence*). I might have a chance of getting into a wireless shop just near us at home. My father knows the man, and he's thinking it over.

Cornelius. Good. You've got your reference from us?

Lawrence. Yes, sir. And thank you very much.

Cornelius (*turning away* R.). And good luck with the wireless.

LAWRENCE (*coming down to* CORNELIUS). Thank you, sir. I—I hope you'll be all right, sir.

CORNELIUS (*turning to* LAWRENCE—*gravely*). Thank you, Lawrence. I think I shall be all right. Good-bye.

LAWRENCE (*shakily*). Good-bye, sir. (*He shakes hands with* CORNELIUS, *blows his nose and crosses below the table for his hat and coat.*)

(CORNELIUS *goes into the other room.* LAWRENCE *hastily gets into his overcoat and hat.* BIDDLE *and* MISS PORRIN *leave their work and come forward.*)

BIDDLE (C., *above the table*). I hope I'll see you again some time, Lawrence.

LAWRENCE (*crossing* C. *to* BIDDLE). I hope so too, Mr. Biddle.

BIDDLE (*shaking hands*). And just remember—that attention to work is the secret of progress.

LAWRENCE (*earnestly*). I shan't forget—not if the work's anything to do with wireless. (*He turns to the door* L.)

(BIDDLE *returns to his desk.*)

MISS PORRIN. Good-bye, Lawrence. We *have* been good friends, haven't we, even though we *have* had our little quarrels?

LAWRENCE (*in a bluff, manly tone*). Yes, Miss Porrin, of course we have. (*He shakes hands.*) Good-bye.

MISS PORRIN. And very good luck. (*She returns to her desk.*)

LAWRENCE (*moving down to* JUDY). Good-bye, Miss Evison.

JUDY (*standing up and smiling at him*). Good-bye, Lawrence. (*She holds out her hand.*)

LAWRENCE (*after looking at her an embarrassed second*). And— and I do think—you're awfully pretty.

(*He hastily wrings the hand she extends, then rushes out.*)

JUDY (*amused*). Sweet!

(*She covers her typewriter, gathers up her letters and envelopes and goes into the private office.* MISS PORRIN *looks up alertly and watches* JUDY, *then, picking up an account book and a few papers, obviously as an excuse to follow her, goes out after her. Meanwhile* BIDDLE *closes his books and tidies up wearily, yawning, etc. When the girls are gone, he changes his office coat by the desk, then crosses for his overcoat, first putting the box of cigars on the table* C. *He carefully puts on his overcoat, puts down his hat by the cigar-box he is taking home, then brings out his pipe, already charged, and lights it.*)

CORNELIUS (*coming out from the private office and letting the door close behind him*). Biddle—oh, are you going?

BIDDLE (L. *of table* C.). Well, I was feeling a bit tired, Mr. Cornelius. But if there's anything else you want me to do to-night, I'll stay.

CORNELIUS. No, no, my dear chap, not necessary at all.

BIDDLE (*after a pause*). I'll come down in the morning and just finish clearing up.

CORNELIUS (*sharply*). No, don't do that.

BIDDLE (*rather surprised*). Oh—all right, Mr. Cornelius. Monday then.

CORNELIUS. No, not Monday. Make it Tuesday.

BIDDLE. Tuesday?

CORNELIUS. Yes. Go away for the week-end, Biddle.

BIDDLE. But I never go away for the week-end——

CORNELIUS. Go down and see that daughter of yours in South Devon. Then you can begin making your arrangements. What sort of business are they in?

BIDDLE. It's her husband's business. Men's outfitting—you know, socks and shirts and collars, all that kind of thing. He's got a nice little business there—the only shop of that kind in the town—and he wants to expand—buy the shop next door.

CORNELIUS. And then you'll help him to sell his socks and shirts and collars, eh?

BIDDLE. I shall have a try.

CORNELIUS. You'll have to learn how to reach up—in one swift continuous flowing movement, Biddle—for all those green and yellow shiny cardboard boxes they have, and then spread them along the counter. "Something in this style, perhaps, sir," you'll say. "We're selling a lot of these this summer." And there they'll be—shiny cardboard boxes—socks and shirts and collars—all in a row. And you'll enjoy it. You'll enjoy every bit of it. Smoking your pipe over the plan for next season's campaign. Spending your weekly half-day holiday looking for the early primroses and violets. You'll be a chief among the elders in that part of South Devon. And you'll play such a devilish game of chess that they'll have to bring a Presbyterian minister specially from Cornwall to beat you. (*Coming down to below* R. *of table.*) I've told you before, Biddle—and I'll tell you again now, for the last time—you're a lucky fellow, a very lucky fellow.

BIDDLE (*laughing*). Sounds like it, Mr. Cornelius, when you put it that way. I'll look in on Tuesday, then. Will you be here, sir?

CORNELIUS (*quietly*). No, I shan't be here.

BIDDLE (*rather taken aback*). Oh!

CORNELIUS. There's nothing more for me to do, is there?

BIDDLE. No—only I didn't—I mean, are you going away?

CORNELIUS. Yes, I'm going away.

BIDDLE (*gently, coming down* L. *of the table*). I expect you want to get away from here, Mr. Cornelius?

CORNELIUS. Yes.

BIDDLE. I know it's been a big strain—Mr. Murrison—and everything——
CORNELIUS. Yes.
BIDDLE (*quickly*). But he didn't know what he was doing, Mr. Cornelius. You mustn't think about it. He was—he was mad—and he just picked up the revolver——
CORNELIUS. No, you're wrong, Biddle. You heard what I said to that woman a few minutes ago. He knew what he was doing. He was sane then. That was the real Bob Murrison.
BIDDLE (*gravely*). I don't like to think that.
CORNELIUS. Why? He saw a chance of slipping out—quickly, decently—and he took it. That poor gibbering fool we saw wasn't Bob Murrison. But it was Bob himself who destroyed him. Came back from—from somewhere—to do it.

(BIDDLE *shakes his head*.)

Biddle, I've been thinking a lot about this lately. One thing puzzled me. I've never believed in this going on and on. I've always thought that when you were dead, that was the end of you. But this—suicide business—somehow doesn't fit in with that. Something inside you, we'll say, compels you to pick up a revolver, pull the trigger——
BIDDLE (*distressed*). Mr. Cornelius—please—don't go on. Leave it alone. Don't think about it.
CORNELIUS (*calmer now*). No, that's all right, my dear fellow. Listen. Something inside you—your will, or whatever it is—compels you to pick up a revolver, pull the trigger, and destroy yourself. But how can you destroy the whole of yourself, Biddle? That's what puzzles me.
BIDDLE. You can't.
CORNELIUS. I can understand that you could destroy a part of yourself, just as you could cut off a finger or a leg. But that something inside you that says, "I've had enough of this. I'm going," *that* can't be destroyed. It must go on existing somewhere, mustn't it?
BIDDLE. Yes, Mr. Cornelius. I've been taught that all my life. That's why I say that suicide's terribly wrong——
CORNELIUS (*sharply*). No, I won't have that.
BIDDLE (*impressively*). Terribly wrong.
CORNELIUS. I tell you, that's all eye-wash. We like to pretend that suicides are cowards when all the time we know damned well they're not. We condemn them because they walk out while we still stay fiddling and frigging behind. They annoy us because they call our bluff.
BIDDLE (*sharply*). No.
CORNELIUS. Yes. They won't have life on any terms. We will —like those people who, because they've paid for a meal, will eat any muck. We linger on and on in the bit of light that's left—

calling it *sticking* it—when all the time we're simply frightened of the jump into the dark.

BIDDLE. No, Mr. Cornelius. You're a cleverer man than I am. But you're all wrong about this. You're not thinking straight.

CORNELIUS. I'm trying to, Biddle.

BIDDLE. If you'll excuse me saying so, you're talking like a man who's tired and a bit sick. After all, who are we to say what life is and what it's worth ?

CORNELIUS. We know what it's offered us.

BIDDLE. We know the bit we've taken, that's all. *You* ought to realize that, Mr. Cornelius.

CORNELIUS. Why *me* specially, Biddle ?

BIDDLE. Well, sir, you've always seemed to me to be interested in all kinds of things——

CORNELIUS (*ruefully*). At a distance.

(*There is a pause.*)

BIDDLE. Is it good-bye for the present then, Mr. Cornelius ?
CORNELIUS. I think it is.

(MISS PORRIN *comes in from the private office and shuts the door behind her. She stands just inside quietly. The other two ignore her.*)

You're a lucky fellow, but you deserve to be. (*Shaking hands.*) Good-bye, Biddle.

BIDDLE. Good-bye, Mr. Cornelius. Good night, Miss Porrin.

(*He goes.* CORNELIUS *goes to the window* L. *and looks out silently for a moment, then draws the blind.* MISS PORRIN *goes to her desk.*)

CORNELIUS. Now then, Miss Porrin, time you were off, isn't it ?

MISS PORRIN (*timidly, coming down below her desk to* CORNELIUS). Mr. Cornelius, I should like to tell you how—how happy I've been here working with you.

CORNELIUS (*rather surprised, but gently*). Have you ? (*He steps towards her.*)

MISS PORRIN (*eagerly*). Oh, yes. The two offices I worked in before this, I didn't like at all, but I've been really happy here—with you.

CORNELIUS. That's fine, Miss Porrin.

MISS PORRIN. And I know I'll never feel like this about any other place——

CORNELIUS (*rather brusquely*). Of course you will. Feel much better. Enormous offices, all glass and metal and light, open at ten and closing at four. That's what you'll have soon, Miss Porrin. Much better than this. Can't compare them.

MISS PORRIN. No. It'll never be the same. And if you're going to stay here, I'd like to stay on too—to help you.

CORNELIUS. Very good of you, but really, there's nothing you can do. I've practically finished now.

(*She looks at him beseechingly.*)

MISS PORRIN. If you have finished—if you are going now—I wondered—if you'd like to talk to me.
CORNELIUS (*bewildered*). Talk to you?
MISS PORRIN (*eagerly*). Yes, couldn't we go somewhere—to eat and drink and talk—I mean, I feel you're so lonely now, and I am too—and we'd have so much to talk about—wouldn't we? having been here together so long. And I'm so sorry about everything. Please, couldn't we?

(CORNELIUS *shakes his head and moves down to beside* JUDY'S *desk.*)

Or, if you didn't want to talk, we could just sit quietly somewhere. I wouldn't mind. I'd like it. Couldn't we?
CORNELIUS (*gently, turning to her*). I'm afraid we couldn't, though it's nice of you to suggest it, very nice. But——
MISS PORRIN (*trying to hide her distress*). No, it doesn't matter. You needn't try to explain.
CORNELIUS. I was only going to say that I've still some things to do here. Some of them are rather—important. I'm sorry.
MISS PORRIN (*going towards the telephone*). It doesn't matter. (*She starts to dial a number.*)
CORNELIUS. Good-bye, Miss Porrin.
MISS PORRIN (*her back to him, muffled*). Good-bye.

(*He looks at her a moment. She is now dialling a number, and trying to control herself. He goes into the private office, closing the door behind him. She is now quietly crying.*)

(*Quietly, trying to control her voice, into the telephone.*) Is that you, Rose? Miss Porrin. Just—just tell them I shan't be staying out —after all. No, it's nothing. I've got—I've got a headache. No, nothing to eat, just some tea——

(JUDY *comes out of the private office with the letters sealed in envelopes. She closes the door behind her and goes across to her desk.*)

I'll be going straight to bed.

(*She puts down the receiver, goes up to the alcove and dabs at her face and is not able to stifle a choking sob.* JUDY *goes up for her coat and hat, then comes down to the desk again for her bag, then moves to the table* C. *She looks at* MISS PORRIN *curiously as* MISS PORRIN *slowly goes to put her things on.*)

JUDY (*quietly*). What's the matter? (*She is* R. *of table* C., *powdering.*)
MISS PORRIN (*putting on her things*). Nothing.

(JUDY *puts her coat on, but places her hat and gloves, etc., on the table.* MISS PORRIN *comes to* L.C. *and stares at her fixedly.*)

JUDY (*smiling, but not unkindly*). Well?
MISS PORRIN (*in low tense voice*). I wish I didn't hate you so much. I've never hated anybody like this before.
JUDY. And you've no right to hate me. What have I done?
MISS PORRIN. Lots of things.
JUDY. What things?
MISS PORRIN. That isn't it.
JUDY. Please tell me why. I don't hate you. I don't hate anybody. As a matter of fact, I don't even dislike you, although you've been unfriendly to me ever since I came here. I've been—rather sorry for you.
MISS PORRIN. Why should you be sorry for me? You're only a child yet, a silly child. You don't really know anything.
JUDY. That's stupid, you know, Miss Porrin. I may be years younger than you, but I'm not a child. I believe I'm more a grown-up person than you are.
MISS PORRIN (*wildly*). Because you're young and pretty now—you think it's going to be always like this. It isn't—(*breaking down*) it isn't, it isn't. (*She turns away.*)
JUDY (*distressed, trying to console her*). Miss Porrin, don't—don't please.
MISS PORRIN (*clutching, urgently*). Listen, forget what I said. That doesn't matter now. Only one thing does matter. He mustn't be so quiet, so unhappy. I'm frightened. He oughtn't to be like that. Stay with him if he wants you to. You see, I ask you to, I don't care what I say now. I'm thinking about him. He's a man. He's different. Please——

(*The private office door has opened and* CORNELIUS *is seen standing there.* MISS PORRIN *gives him one look, then hurries out.* JUDY *and* CORNELIUS *stand perfectly still until there is heard the sound of a distant door slamming. Then* CORNELIUS *turns back to switch off the private office light, after which he comes in and closes the door quietly behind him. Meanwhile* JUDY *has gone to the window, and looks down into the street. She comes away and looks at* CORNELIUS *as he approaches.*)

CORNELIUS (*at the door* R.—*awkwardly*). I suppose you ought to go now.
JUDY. Yes.

(*There is a pause. She returns to* L. *of table for her bag and gloves.*)

CORNELIUS. How old are you?
JUDY (*smiling*). Must you know?
CORNELIUS (*hastily*). No, no. (*Crossing to* R. *of table.*) What does it matter? Whatever it is, I'm twice it. You think of a number and I double it.

JUDY (*smiling*). And then I shall take away the number I first thought of—and myself with it. (*She turns away.*)
CORNELIUS. What do you do when you're at home?
JUDY. Oh!—read—sew a bit, not much—listen to the wireless. The usual things. Quite commonplace.
CORNELIUS (*staring at her, musingly*). Perhaps you are quite commonplace—really.
JUDY (*promptly*). No, I'm not. I'm *really* rather special.
CORNELIUS (*absently*). Yes?
JUDY (*indecisively*). I think I ought to go. (*She moves towards her desk* L.)
CORNELIUS. No, please don't go. You've plenty of time. You've no idea how much time you have—years and years and years. (*He moves to below* L. *of table.*)
JUDY (*laughing*). Not to-night, I haven't. Somebody's waiting for me. (*She leans against her table.*)
CORNELIUS (*making conversation*). Have you liked it here?
JUDY. Parts of it.
CORNELIUS. Biddle's a nice fellow, isn't he?
JUDY. Yes. I like Mr. Biddle.
CORNELIUS (*lamely, moving up* L. *of table to above it*). Very good chap. (*He turns round to her.*)
JUDY (*with mock official manner*). And—is that all, Mr. Cornelius? (*She goes up to him,* L. *of* C.)
CORNELIUS. No, it isn't all. It isn't any. It's nothing. It's nothing. I haven't begun to talk yet. I don't know how to begin. Something happened that very first morning you came here. It's not long ago——
JUDY. A fortnight last Monday, to be exact.
CORNELIUS. Not much happened then, perhaps. But afterwards—only a day or two—just before we had the meeting here—and I came in and you were singing.
JUDY. I remember. You were very nice about that.
CORNELIUS (*almost to himself*). It's as if it's been dark here ever since then—and you carried a little light with you. When you came in, it wasn't so dark. There was a light round your head. And the song has never stopped. It's a long time since I felt like this, a long, long time. That's why I can't tell you properly. It's —it's a good record, but the gramophone's old and rusty. I'm sorry.
JUDY (*putting out a hand*). I'm sorry too.
CORNELIUS (*eagerly*). Are you? (*Taking her hand.*) How small and clear you are—like the flame of a candle! (*He pauses, then laughs shortly and harshly.*)
JUDY. What does that mean?
CORNELIUS (*moving* R.). I was thinking—here's the good old situation they're so fond of in the magazine stories and the comic papers. The business man keeps the typist in the office after hours to make love to her. (*He is down* R.)

JUDY (*sharply*). No. I know it's not like that at all. (*She moves slightly towards him.*)
CORNELIUS (*harshly*). But it is. I'm a business man—or I was. You're a typist. This is an office. And it's late. And I'm making love to you.
JUDY. You're not. Not in that way.
CORNELIUS. Yes, I am. In that way, in every way.
JUDY. Oh—why do you say that? Can't you see you're spoiling everything?
CORNELIUS (*wonderingly*). Am I?
JUDY. Yes. Please stop. You're only hurting yourself.
CORNELIUS. That's nothing. Tell me what a fool I am—now, after all this time—to fall in love again, like a boy. Yes, like a boy. (*He goes towards her.*)
JUDY. You can't expect me to tell you that.
CORNELIUS (*eagerly*). Can't I? (*He catches her hands as she smiles and shakes her head.*) Why, Judy, then—little Judy—is this real?

(JUDY *is directly* C. *below the table;* CORNELIUS R. *of her. He tries to kiss her, but deliberately she turns her face away so that his kiss falls lamely on her cheek. He withdraws, bewildered and disappointed.*)

Oh!
JUDY (*distressed*). I'm sorry. I ought to have told you. It isn't that I don't like you. I do. But—you see—I'm in love with somebody too.
CORNELIUS. I see.
JUDY. He's outside now—waiting for me. That's why—I couldn't, you see.
CORNELIUS. And you're in love with him?
JUDY. Yes. I know I ought to have told you at once. It wasn't fair to you.

(*To her astonishment, he suddenly laughs, not without bitterness, but still—a genuine laugh.*)

CORNELIUS. *It wasn't fair to me!* I said I was behaving like a boy, and now that very phrase takes me back thirty years. Technical College boys and High School girls, parties and sets of lancers, and somebody saying, "It wasn't fair of you, Alice, not to tell Tom you were going with Frank." My God, I've asked for it, and I've got it. (*He laughs again and goes up* R. *of table.*)
JUDY (*annoyed*). I think I'd better go. (*She moves away to the door, then turns to him.*) I stayed—and listened—because I liked you and I was sorry.
CORNELIUS (*not unkindly*). No other reason?
JUDY. Yes. Because I'm a girl, and I knew what you were

E

feeling, and I wanted to hear what you'd say to me. Any girl would.

CORNELIUS. That's honest of you.

JUDY. I am honest. More honest than you are.

CORNELIUS. Oh?

JUDY (*with force*). Yes. (*Crossing to* C. *above the table.*) If you meant what you said to me a few minutes ago, you shouldn't pretend now—because it's all no use—that you weren't serious. That's cowardly and hateful.

CORNELIUS (*gravely*). My dear, it isn't so simple as that. I've been as honest as possible with you all the time. It's too late for anything else. And if I offended you a moment ago, I'm sorry, Judy.

JUDY (*smiling at him*). All right. And I'm sorry too.

CORNELIUS (*sitting* R. *of the table*). There's one thing I'd like you to do for me. If this young man of yours is waiting outside, I wish you'd call him in for a moment.

JUDY (*rather puzzled*). You'd like to see him?

CORNELIUS. Yes. After all, that's not much to ask, is it?

JUDY (*hesitating*). No—only—all right, I'll see if he's out there.

(*She crosses and opens the down stage window* L., *and can be heard giving a singing call down into the street below. Then she cries* "Eric, come up here," *waits a moment, then returns to* CORNELIUS.)

CORNELIUS. And you're in love with him?

JUDY (*at the window*). Yes.

CORNELIUS. He's a very lucky young man. And he's in love with you?

JUDY. Yes. (*Crossing back to table* C.) We adore each other. We want to get married as soon as he's settled down in his present job. I'm longing to be married. I'd hate to go on years and years, working in offices—like poor Miss Porrin.

CORNELIUS. I'm afraid Miss Porrin didn't like you.

JUDY. Of course not. She was jealous—poor thing.

CORNELIUS. And now it's my turn—poor thing.

JUDY. You don't sound very jealous.

CORNELIUS. I don't think I am. Rather sad, perhaps. And very curious.

JUDY. I don't like that.

CORNELIUS. I shall never see you again. You must let me spend a minute or two guessing what the rest of your life's going to be like. And I think I hear it coming.

(CORNELIUS *rises and moves* R. *down stage.* JUDY *turns to the door, expectantly. There is a tap, then* ERIC SHEFFORD *enters. He is wearing an overcoat and a spotted silk muffler, and carries his hat. He stops when he sees* CORNELIUS.)

JUDY (*going over to* SHEFFORD *at the door and taking his arm*).

Hello, Eric. Come in. Mr. Cornelius wanted to meet you. This is Eric Shefford. (*She leads* SHEFFORD *to* L.C. *She is* L. *of him.*)

CORNELIUS (*turning round—almost involuntarily*). My God, it's the twister.

JUDY. The what?

SHEFFORD (*sulkily*). All right. I didn't come here to be insulted.

CORNELIUS. We know that. Nobody goes anywhere to be insulted.

JUDY. But do you know each other?

CORNELIUS (*dryly*). Only slightly. A business acquaintance.

JUDY. But why didn't you tell me, Eric?

SHEFFORD. It wasn't of any importance. I'd only called here twice.

CORNELIUS. That's all. We did a little business together, and then somehow I quarrelled with his company, the Excelsior Transport, whose banner has a strange device.

SHEFFORD. I didn't know you were here, else I wouldn't have come in.

JUDY. I want to know what happened? (*She crosses below the table to* CORNELIUS.)

CORNELIUS. It doesn't matter. He'll tell you some time.

JUDY. What did you call him?

SHEFFORD. He called me a twister, if you must know, Judy.

JUDY (*from one to the other*). Why?

CORNELIUS. Never mind now.

JUDY (*going to* SHEFFORD). Why?

SHEFFORD (*quickly, rather desperately*). He thinks I deliberately misled him about some rates I quoted, and got the business under false pretences.

JUDY. And did you?

(SHEFFORD *is silent.*)

Eric!

SHEFFORD. Yes, I suppose I did. Though I didn't do anything illegal. But I'd got to get some business, to keep the job. You know what it was like, I told you, Judy. I was desperate. I'm sorry, Mr. Cornelius, but you don't understand what it's like trying to keep a job like that. The competition's terrible. I know I was wrong——

CORNELIUS. All right, all right. It's done with now. (*He sits* R. *of table* C.)

JUDY. Is it?

SHEFFORD. But, Judy, you can't blame me. I was doing it for your sake. And you know what a time I'd had before.

JUDY. Yes, I know, Eric.

SHEFFORD. I'm sorry I didn't tell you before. Are you coming along now?

Judy (*hesitating*). Just a minute, Eric, please.

Shefford. Oh—all right—but I've been hanging about down there——

Judy. I know. I'm sorry. (*She takes his arm and leads him to the door.*) But please wait outside, I shan't be two minutes.

(*He goes. They wait a moment.* Judy *returns to above* L. *of table and faces* Cornelius.)

Now tell me what you're thinking.

(*He shakes his head.*)

I'm not afraid. You can say what you like. It won't make any difference to me. I know him. You don't—really.

Cornelius. No, of course I don't, my dear.

Judy. I know he can be very stupid, very weak, sometimes. I know we may have all kinds of trouble.

Cornelius (*gravely*). I think you may.

Judy. But it can't be helped. You see, I love him.

Cornelius. Yes, I see.

Judy. You think I'm very young and silly now, don't you? But I'm not. I know my life with Eric isn't going to be easy, I know it far better than you do. But it's my life. I wouldn't run away from it. Even though you're a girl—and a girl in love—you need courage, a special sort of courage, if you're going to live properly. My sister has it. I have it too.

Cornelius. Yes, you have. I'll wish you luck. And do it properly. (*Rising and picking up* Murrison's *flask.*) See. I'll drink your health. His too, if you like.

Judy. I don't understand you.

Cornelius. That's as it should be. Otherwise I'd have lived these extra five-and-twenty years of mine for nothing. (*He moves away slightly up stage.*) A solemn toast. (*In manner of toastmaster.*) My lords, ladies and gentlemen, see that your glasses are charged, and pray silence for your chairman, the Wrong Dishonourable James Frederick Cornelius, Knight of the Ancient Order of Near Bankrupts.

(Judy *laughs. His manner suddenly changes.*)

May you always be brave and happy, Judy, always be as clear and beautiful as the flame of a candle.

(Judy *moves away* L. Cornelius *drinks. Then he sits down at the table, and she stands facing him and the window at back, very clearly seen.*)

No, don't move. Don't speak.

Judy (*softly, uncertainly*). I wouldn't find it easy—if I wanted to.

Cornelius (*putting his head in his hands as he stares*). That song —how does it go?

(*She sings the tiny song she sang in Act II, and he remains motionless, lumped on the table, his head down. There is a pause when she has done. Then* JUDY *goes round and up stage to behind* COR-NELIUS. *She puts her arms round him and her cheek against him. As he moves she snatches up her things and runs off quickly.*)

(*Very quietly, without raising his head.*) Good-bye, Judy.
JUDY. Good-bye.

(*She disappears. Very slowly after staring at the door he rises. He gives a glance at the window, then moves like a man in a dream. He holds up the flask so that he can see a reflection of himself in the silver base of it.*)

CORNELIUS (*quietly to his reflection*). You silly old fool!

(*He rises, gets ink, pen and paper from* BIDDLE'S *desk, then returns to the table and starts writing. There is a noise. Then the door is slowly opened, and* MRS. ROBERTS *enters. She is rather breathless. She leaves her bag by* MISS PORRIN'S *desk.*)

What is it?
MRS. ROBERTS. I just called to see if Mr. Biddle had left me my week's money in my envelope, and to pick up one or two of my bits o' cleaning things. (*She goes over to* BIDDLE'S *desk for the envelope, then goes to the cupboard to collect the cleaning things. While at the cupboard she takes the empty whisky bottle and puts it in her apron.*) All packing up, eh? (*She takes the things across* L. *and puts them in her bag.*)
CORNELIUS. Yes, finished.
MRS. ROBERTS. What happened to you, then? Did you go bankrupt, or what?
CORNELIUS. We came to a private agreement with our creditors.
MRS. ROBERTS (*buttoning up her coat*). Well, I wish to God I could come to one with mine. Are you going away?
CORNELIUS. Yes.
MRS. ROBERTS. I wish I could get away.
CORNELIUS. Where would you go to?
MRS. ROBERTS (*crossing to* CORNELIUS). I've always had a fancy for Eastbourne.
CORNELIUS. I don't think you'd like it.
MRS. ROBERTS. If I could only have my feet up most o' the morning and afternoon and no cleaning and have a nice tea on a fancy tray, then go out and see a bit o' life in the evening, anywhere would do me. (*She goes back to the cupboard* R. *and shuts the door.*)
CORNELIUS (*reflectively*). I suppose women are really tougher than men.
MRS. ROBERTS. I should think they are! If women was as soft as men when a bit o' trouble came—there'd be nothing here but a graveyard soon.

CORNELIUS. It isn't much else here now. Millions of people, none of them real, and those that are real are mostly in graveyards now.

MRS. ROBERTS. Come, come, Mr. Cornelius, I'm not worrying, and I can give you a year or two.

CORNELIUS. You can't. That's the trouble. Nobody can. And I want a few. I've wasted so many.

MRS. ROBERTS. Where?

CORNELIUS. Here, among other places.

MRS. ROBERTS (*indignantly*). Why, you're not going to start grumbling now—are you?—just because you've spent a few years sitting here in a nice office, with other people waiting on you, and three good meals a day and anything else you liked? Gertcha! You don't know you're born. (*She goes and picks up her bag.*)

CORNELIUS. But I do. That's the point. I think a lot of people don't, and it's a bit of luck for them. I know I'm born—when it's too late.

MRS. ROBERTS. Well, my motto is, it's never too late. (*Crossing to* CORNELIUS.) You look after yourself, Mr. Cornelius. Good-night. (*She moves towards the door.*)

CORNELIUS. Good-night.

MRS. ROBERTS. Good-night.

(*She looks at him for a moment, troubled, then goes out.* CORNELIUS *rises and takes out the revolver, breaks it to see if it is loaded and then puts it on the table. He goes to the door and locks it, throwing the key away on the floor. He then switches off the lights, opens the window, and returns to the table to pick up the revolver. He is attracted by sounds of laughter and a banjo and his face lights up as he listens. Suddenly he becomes decisive, looks at the revolver and says,* "No—no, Bob," *then drops the revolver and picks up the big ledger from the table.*)

CORNELIUS. After a week in the Indian village—(*he speaks jerkily all the time, though with gathering force*)—we decided to take the track into the clouds—to find—among those heights——

(*He hurls the ledger with such force that the door is smashed clean open, so that he can walk through, repeating triumphantly.*)

—the lost city of the Incas.

CURTAIN.

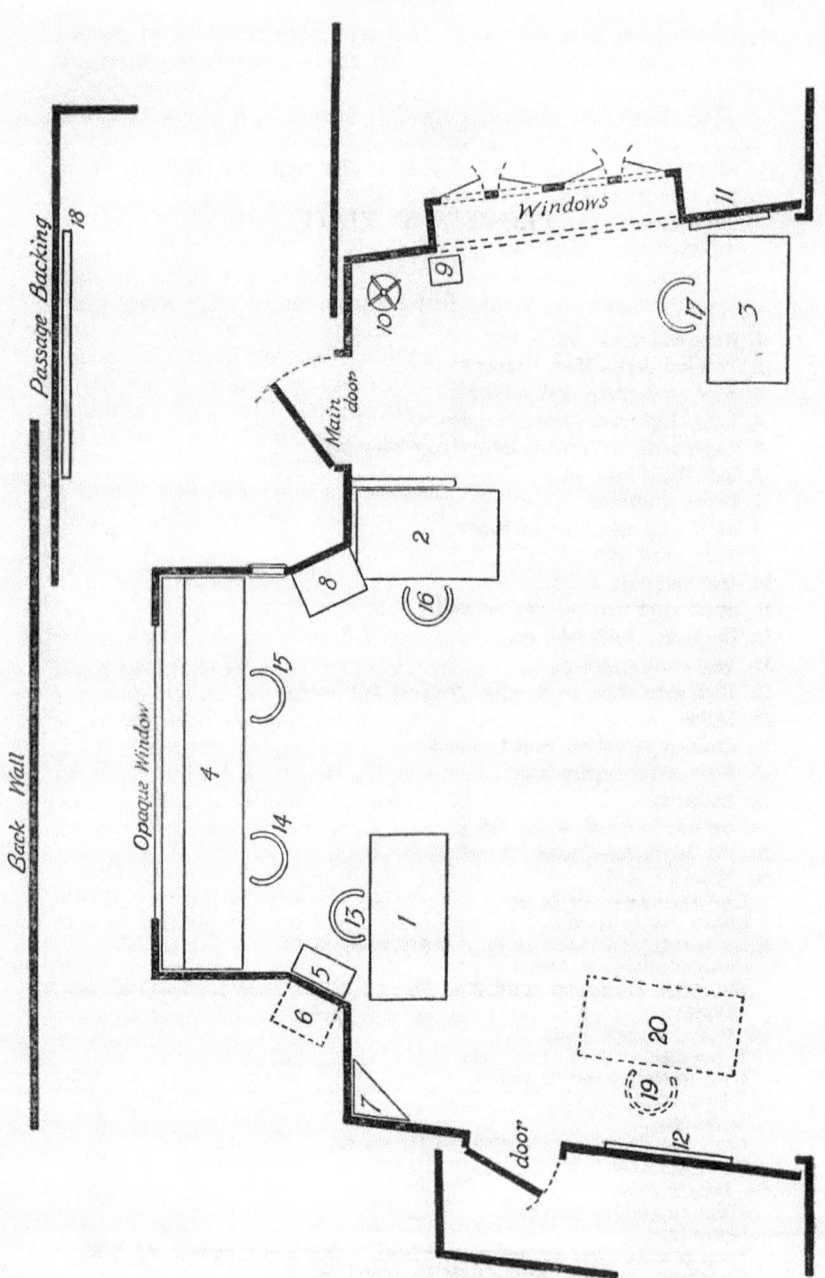

PROPERTY PLOT

ACT I

1. Knee-hole desk—BIDDLE's.
2. Pedestal desk—MISS PORRIN's.
3. New typewriting desk—JUDY's.
4. Long, high desk—length of alcove.
5. Small table, with old-fashioned copying-press.
6. Safe, built into set.
7. Corner cupboard.
8. Shelf with telephone exchange.
9. Very small table.
10. Hat and coat stand.
11. Small cupboard hanging on wall.
12. Cupboard, built into set.
13. Bentwood armchair.
14. High stool with back—upholstered in red leather.
15. Ditto.
16. Chair—upholstered in red leather.
17. New swivel typing chair.
18. Radiator.
19. Swivel chair—off R. for Act I.
20. Writing-table—CORNELIUS—off R. for Act I.

On BIDDLE's *Desk.*
  Used blotting-paper in pad.
  Inkpot (ready to fill).
  Letter-tray, with loose sheet of paper under tray.
  Business letters in drawer.
  Pen, office notepaper, envelopes, etc.
  Telephone.

On MISS PORRIN's *Desk.*
  Typewriter.
  Used blotting-paper in pad.
  Inkpot (ready to fill).
  Letter-tray.
  Pens, pencils, office notepaper, envelopes, etc.
  Calendar—13th.

On JUDY's *Desk.*
  Silent typewriter (covered).
  Letter-tray.
  Pens, pencils, office notepaper, envelopes, typing paper, carbon paper, etc.
  Shorthand notebook, with elastic band and pencil.
  Letter-tray.

CORNELIUS.

On Desk in Alcove.
  Large in-ledger.
  Large bottle of ink.
  Inkpot.
  Pens, pencils, etc.
  Clean blotting-paper for pads.
  Ledgers, files, etc.

On Shelf up L.
  Telephone.
  Exchange.
  Telegraph forms and pencil.

In Safe.
  Cash-box with money (three large coins in silver—7*s.* 6*d.*)
  Stamp-book.
  Stamps.
  Bank book.

In Cupboard down R.
  Broom.
  Various cleaning materials—"Bluebell," floor polish, etc.
  Stationery—boxes of notepaper, envelopes, carbons and other typewriting materials, etc.

On Hat-stand.
  MRS. ROBERTS' coat, hat and bag.

On Peg by BIDDLE'S *Desk.*
  BIDDLE'S office coat.

On Floor.
  Coal in newspaper below BIDDLE'S desk.
  Pail O.

Off Stage R.
  Table ; with blotter, letter-tray, inkpot, pens, pencils, etc., office notepaper, envelopes.
  Swivel chair.
  Waste-paper basket.
  Index cards.

Off Stage up L.
  Duster for MRS. ROBERTS.
  German book for MISS PORRIN.
  "Morning Post" for BIDDLE.
  Rugs for RUG-SELLER.
  Bag for PAPER-TOWEL MAN.
  Cablegram for COLEMAN.
  Fitted case containing soap, shaving-cream, etc., for YOUNG WOMAN.
  Attaché-case containing stationery for EX-OFFICER.
  Attaché-case with library-book for JUDY.
  Telegram.
  Book wrapped up.
  Letters.

Letters in basket behind door.
  1. Solicitor's letter.
  2. Shaw and Johnson with cheque.
  3. Excelsior Transport Company.
  4. Czecho-Slovachia (hand-written).
  5. and 6. Crematorium.
  N.B.—3 goes to MISS PORRIN'S desk, the others to BIDDLE'S desk. Also ordinary letters for both desks.

74 CORNELIUS.
ACT II

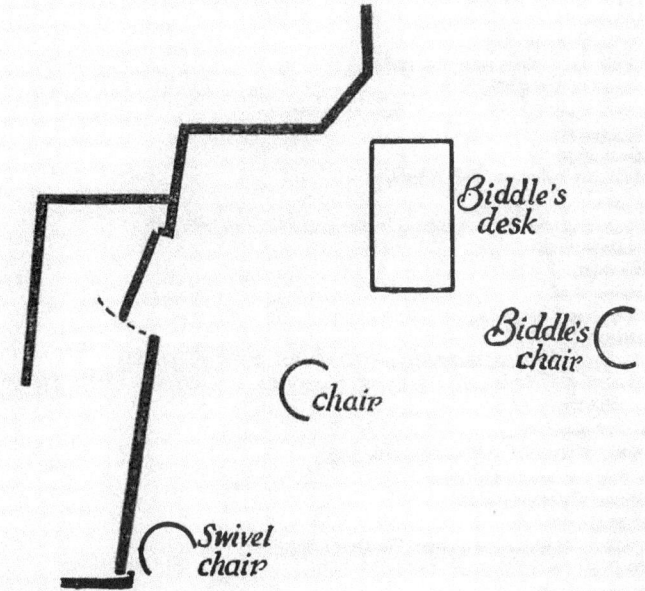

On BIDDLE'S *Desk*.
    As in Act I.
    Telephone up stage on desk.
On MISS PORRIN'S *Desk*.
    As in Act I.
    Statement for CORNELIUS.
    No letter-tray.
    Change calendar to 15th.
On JUDY'S *Desk*.
    Typewriter (uncovered).
    Flap up.
    Office paper and envelopes set.
    Letter-tray L. of typewriter.
    Paper fasteners, etc.
    JUDY's case R. of desk.
Off Stage R.
    Ham sandwich and glass of stout for CORNELIUS.
    Two chairs.
    Revolver for MURRISON.
Off Stage L.
    Nine cups of tea and plate with cake on tray.
    Dispatch-case containing two loose-leaf files, eversharp pencil, paper, etc., for SCHWEIG.
    Pamphlets for PROPHET.
    Visiting card for FLETCHER.
    Folded statement for MORTIMER.
    Leather case containing legal documents tied with pink tape.
    Paper with list of clients for PRITCHET.
    Bags for TAXI-MAN.

ACT III

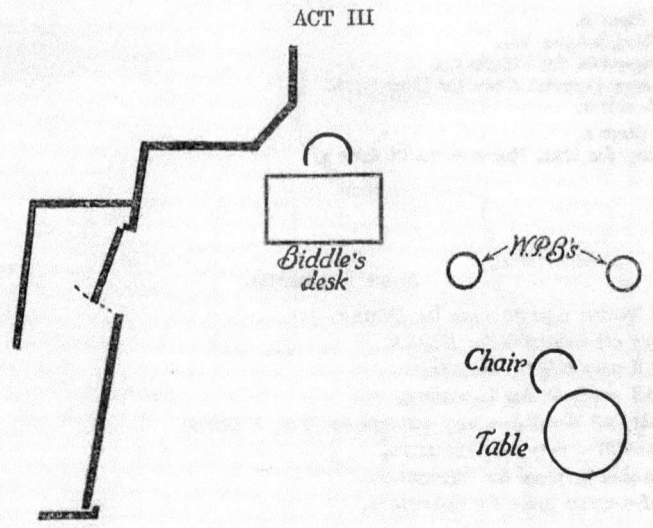

At Round Table C.
   Ledgers, files, etc., in neat piles under table.
   Up stage of table two large waste-paper baskets.
   Two or three ledgers on table, including ledger for breaking door.
On BIDDLE'S *Desk*.
   Ledgers, files, papers.
   Wages for MRS. ROBERTS in envelope.
   One sheet of notepaper and pen and ink in drawer for CORNELIUS.
On MISS PORRIN'S *Desk*.
   Blotting-paper, ink, etc., struck.
   Calendar—31st.
   Pile of ledgers on floor below desk.
On JUDY'S *Desk*.
   Typewriter (uncovered).
   One letter and thick paper in tray, and headed paper and thick sheet in
      typewriter.
   Opened letters.
On Desk in Alcove.
   Piles of ledgers and files.
On Hat-stand.
   LAWRENCE'S coat and hat.
   BIDDLE'S coat and hat.
   MISS PORRIN'S coat and hat.
   JUDY'S coat and hat.
On Peg by BIDDLE'S *Desk*.
   BIDDLE'S coat.
On the Press.
   Newspaper.
In Cupboard down R.
   Apron, bag and cleaning things.
   Whisky-bottle—nearly empty.
   Glass and syphon—nearly empty.
   No stationery.

Off Stage R.
　Files, ledgers, etc.
　Cigar-box for CORNELIUS.
　Large personal diary for CORNELIUS.
　Revolver.
Off Stage L.
　Key for MRS. ROBERTS to fit door L.

HAND PROPERTIES.

Old leather cigarette-case for BIDDLE.
Large old notebook for BIDDLE.
Small notebook for CORNELIUS.
Small notebook for LAWRENCE.
Packet of Woodbines and matches for MRS. ROBERTS.
Ten-shilling note for CORNELIUS.
Two-shilling piece for CORNELIUS.
Half-a-crown piece for CORNELIUS.